Do You KNOW?

ULTIMATE TRIVIA Book

by Guy Robinson

SOURCEBOOKS, INC.
NAPERVILLE, ILLINOIS

Published by Sourcebooks, Inc.
P.O. Box 4410, Naperville, Illinois 60567-4410
(630) 961-3900
Fax: (630) 961-2168
www.sourcebooks.com

ISBN-13: 978-1-4022-1206-2
ISBN-10: 1-4022-1206-2

Printed and bound in Canada
WC 10 9 8 7 6 5 4 3 2 1

Welcome to the Quiz

If you chose this book, or received it as a gift, odds are you have the kind of mind that grabs onto facts and won't let go. They may be weighty facts of history-making, earth-moving importance or quick details that cry out with insignificance and frivolity, but you enjoy reaching into the recesses of your brain and pulling them out on call. You're that kind of person.

What's more, everybody knows it. You're the one everyone calls when they're trying to come up with the name of the janitor who discovered the Watergate break-in or Archie and Edith Bunker's street address. You're expected to know the name of LBJ's ranch, what "just thinking about tomorrow" does for Annie, the names of all seven dwarfs, and who was famous for saying "Kiss my grits!" And you do.

This book is for you.

This is a quiz book with three kinds of questions: those you know, those you once knew but can't quite remember and it's driving you mad, and those you can't answer but you'd really like to know, because, well, that's the kind of person you are. So in these pages you can show your stuff, refresh your memory, and maybe learn something new along the way.

Enjoy it.

—G.R.

Tally Your Score As You Go

This book contains 150 one-page quizzes. Answers worth a specified number of points, from 2 to 100 per question, are upside down at the foot of each page. You're on your honor not to twist the book or your head to sneak a look before you decide on your response.

Many of the questions are in multiple-choice format. Occasionally, more than one choice—or all of them, or none of them—may be correct; keep on your toes. Other questions call for you to come up with the answer without a menu to choose from; if you almost get it right, feel free to take partial credit.

Just below the answers on each page are lines where you can fill in your total for the quiz and keep a running tally. All told, the answers in the book are worth 8,380 points. At the end of the questions, we'll tell you how to evaluate your performance.

Good luck!

Do You Know **WHO**?

Take 2 points for each correct answer. Maximum this page: 10 points!

1. WHO is described as "joy of joys," "my very best friend," and "so fine"?
   a. Claudette
   b. Teen Angel
   c. Rubber Duckie
   d. The Girl That I Marry

2. WHO cleaned house at the Jetsons'?
   a. George and Jane
   b. Judy and Elroy
   c. Rosie the robot
   d. No one—it was a mess

3. WHO offered the wise counsel: "The future's not ours to see"?
   a. Dr. Joyce Brothers, on her TV advice program
   b. Ronald Reagan, in his first inaugural address
   c. Carl Sagan, on *The Tonight Show with Johnny Carson*
   d. Doris Day, in the song "Que Sera Sera"

4. WHO was sued by Texas cattlemen for bad-mouthing beef?
   a. Oprah Winfrey
   b. David Letterman
   c. Ralph Nader
   d. Alec Baldwin

5. WHO was "The Caped Crusader"?
   a. Superman
   b. Batman
   c. Plastic Man
   d. Count Dracula

SCORE FOR THIS TEST: _____ TOTAL SO FAR: _____

Do You Know **WHAT**?

Take 2 points for each correct answer. Maximum this page: 10 points!

1. WHAT was Dumbo the Elephant's unusual talent?
- a. He could sing anything from bass to soprano
- b. He could type with his trunk
- c. He could fly
- d. He could grill a perfect burger

2. WHAT body part do you associate with Vincent Van Gogh?
- a. Finger
- b. Toe
- c. Ear
- d. Nose

3. After you put your left arm in, you put your left arm out. Then you put your left arm in a second time. WHAT next?
- a. You put your left arm out again
- b. You wiggle it at your partner
- c. You put your left leg in
- d. You shake it all about

4. According to the nursery ditty "Sing a Song of Sixpence," while "the king was in his counting house, counting out his money," WHAT was the queen doing?
- a. "The Queen was in the garden, where it's warm and sunny"
- b. "The Queen was in the backyard, playing with her bunny"
- c. "The Queen was in the parlor, eating bread and honey"
- d. "The Queen was in the draperies—she thought it awful funny"

5. In *Public Enemy,* WHAT does James Cagney shove into Mae Clark's face?
- a. His shoe
- b. Her shoe
- c. A slice of pizza
- d. Half a grapefruit

SCORE FOR THIS TEST: _____ TOTAL SO FAR: _____

Do You Know **WHEN**?

Take 2 points for each correct answer. Maximum this page: 10 points!

1. WHEN was Bob Dylan booed at the Newport Folk Festival?
- a. 1963
- b. 1965
- c. 1968
- d. 1988

2. WHEN did Ray Kroc, founder of the McDonald's empire, open his first burger shop?
- a. 1935
- b. 1955
- c. 1965
- d. 1975

3. Every Beatles fan remembers the "Paul is dead" rumors. WHEN did all that start?
- a. 1980
- b. 1975
- c. 1971
- d. 1969

4. WHEN was the first automatic plain-paper copier, the Xerox 914, sold for the first time?
- a. 1939
- b. 1949
- c. 1959
- d. 1969

5. WHEN will the teddy bears' mummies and daddies take them home to bed?
- a. At six o'clock
- b. After the fun
- c. When games are done
- d. When they're too tired to play and eat

SCORE FOR THIS TEST: _____ TOTAL SO FAR: _____

Do You Know **WHERE**?

Take 2 points for each correct answer. Maximum this page: 10 points!

1. WHERE in the writings of Arthur Conan Doyle was the favorite Sherlock Holmes sound bite "Elementary, my dear Watson" first uttered?
- a. *The Hound of the Baskervilles*
- b. *A Study in Scarlet*
- c. None of Doyle's stories
- d. Every one of Doyle's stories

2. WHERE did Edith Piaf get the name Piaf?
- a. It was her mother's maiden name
- b. It was her first husband's name
- c. It was her name at birth
- d. It was a nickname given her by a nightclub owner

4. In the TV series *Will and Grace,* WHERE did the title characters meet?
- a. At a gay bar
- b. At a straight singles bar
- c. In their college dorm
- d. Waiting in line to see *The Rocky Horror Picture Show*

3. WHERE does Nathan Detroit hope to hold "the oldest established permanent floating crap game in New York"—if he can raise the grand needed to pay off the owner?
- a. The Biltmore Garage
- b. The Horn & Hardart Automat
- c. The Bickford Cafeteria
- d. The Havana Hilton

5. WHERE was Arlo Guthrie arrested for littering, as told in "Alice's Restaurant Massacre," his famous talking blues?
- a. Nantucket, Massachusetts
- b. Stockbridge, Massachusetts
- c. Woodstock, New York
- d. Malibu, California

SCORE FOR THIS TEST: _____ TOTAL SO FAR: _____

Do You Know **WHY**?

Take 2 points for each correct answer. Maximum this page: 10 points!

1. WHY did Anne Frank dream of becoming a writer?

a. She wanted to impress the teenage Peter
b. She wanted to live after death through her words
c. She wanted to earn enough money to buy her family's freedom
d. She just couldn't help herself

2. WHY did Jor-El and Lara send their son Kal-El to a distant planet called Earth?

a. Because their planet was doomed
b. So that he could see how others lived before starting his own life
c. To gather specimens of Earth beings for an experiment
d. To visit relatives

3. WHY does a horse tap a front hoof on the ground?

a. He's angry
b. He's content
c. He's hungry
d. He's bored

4. WHY did the *Titanic* sink?

a. There was a major defect in her hull
b. She hit a whale
c. She hit an iceberg
d. She was attacked by an armed pirate vessel

5. WHY did Elvira Gulch take Toto away from Dorothy?

a. The dog got into Ms. Gulch's garden, chased her cat, and bit her
b. Aunty Em promised to give Toto to Ms. Gulch as a birthday present
c. Toto had originally belonged to Ms. Gulch, and she wanted him back
d. She believed Toto was the father of her own dog's puppies, and she wanted to perform a paternity test

SCORE FOR THIS TEST: _____ TOTAL SO FAR: _____

ANSWERS: 1. b, **2.** a (the boy became Superman, of course), **3.** d, **4.** c, **5.** a (*The Wizard of Oz*)

Do You Know **HOW**?

Take 2 points for each correct answer. Maximum this page: 10 points!

1. HOW did Helen Keller lose her sight and hearing?

   a. She was born blind and deaf
   b. She was born blind and lost her hearing from an explosion inside a mine
   c. She lost both senses from an injury suffered when she was thrown by a horse
   d. She lost both senses from a brief but acute illness, possibly scarlet fever

2. In *The Adventures of Tom Sawyer,* after they witness a murder in the grave-yard, HOW do Tom and Huck promise never to tell?

   a. By swearing to God
   b. By swearing on Aunt Polly's life
   c. By signing an oath in blood
   d. By "putting it in the vault"

3. HOW did the rock group Sha Na Na get its name?

   a. From the lyrics to "Get a Job" by the Fleetwoods
   b. From the title of a song by the Del Vikings
   c. From an expression used by drummer Jocko's grandmother
   d. From the shortened form of three band members' names

4. According to a well debunked urban legend, HOW did Cass Elliot of The Mamas & the Papas die?

   a. Mixed Coca-Cola and aspirin
   b. Choked on a ham sandwich
   c. Willed herself to die after the breakup of her marriage
   d. Walked off a bridge in a music-induced trance

5. Hervé Villechaize, who played Tattoo on *Fantasy Island*—HOW did he die?

   a. Shot himself
   b. Murdered by the show's assistant director
   c. Ate bad snails
   d. Fell from a trapeze

SCORE FOR THIS TEST: _____ TOTAL SO FAR: _____

ANSWERS: 1. d, **2.** c, **3.** a, **4.** b (actually, the coroner's autopsy said the singer, weighing nearly 240 pounds, suffered heart failure), **5.** a

Do You Know **WHICH**?

Take 2 points for each correct answer. Maximum this page: 10 points!

1. WHICH dance is done to the count "One, two, one-two-three; one, two, one-two-three?"
   a. Cha-cha-cha
   b. Polka
   c. Mambo
   d. Tango

2. WHICH dates farthest back in history?
   a. Popcorn
   b. Tulips
   c. Cockroaches
   d. Elephants

3. WHICH auto is featured in the movie *Back to the Future?*
   a. Maserati
   b. Bentley
   c. DeLorean
   d. Metropolitan

4. The movie *Arsenic and Old Lace* is about two elderly women with a murderous bent. WHICH of these statements is true?
   a. The perps are identical twins
   b. They serve each victim poisoned chicken noodle soup
   c. All the murders take place at the beach
   d. All the victims are men

5. Without looking at a keyboard, WHICH four letters follow QWERTY?
   a. ASDF
   b. UIOP
   c. HJKL
   d. ZXCV

SCORE FOR THIS TEST: _____ TOTAL SO FAR: _____

Do You Know **WHICH—ODD ONE OUT**?

Take 4 points for each correct answer. Maximum this page: 20 points!

1. WHICH has *never* been a Mr. Potato Head character?
   - a. Santa Spud
   - b. Darth Tater
   - c. The Potato Bandito
   - d. Artoo-Patatoo

2. WHICH *isn't* a member of the Ivy League?
   - a. Columbia
   - b. Harvard
   - c. University of Pennsylvania
   - d. Massachusetts Institute of Technology

3. WHICH early rock star *didn't* die in a plane crash on "The Day the Music Died," February 3, 1959?
   - a. Roy Orbison
   - b. Ritchie Valens
   - c. The Big Bopper
   - d. Buddy Holly

4. For WHICH instrument did Wolfgang Amadeus Mozart *never* write a concerto?
   - a. Trumpet
   - b. Violin
   - c. Bassoon
   - d. Clarinet

5. WHICH character *wasn't* an accomplice of Austin Powers?
   - a. Felicity Shagwell
   - b. Pussy Galore
   - c. Foxxy Cleopatra
   - d. Vanessa Kensington

SCORE FOR THIS TEST: _____ TOTAL SO FAR: _____

Do You Know **FILL-IN QUIZ**?

Take 10 points for each correct answer. Maximum this page: 50 points!

1. John Blutarsky's nickname: _____.

2. City where Rosie Ruiz hopped a train _____.

3. Garnered several "worst actresses" awards in the eighties, and pushed Dubonnet in a series of commercials: _____ _____.

4. Robot in *The Day the Earth Stood Still:* _____.

5. Sent a Native American to the Oscar ceremony to decline an award and chew out the academy: _____ _____.

SCORE FOR THIS TEST: _____ TOTAL SO FAR: _____

ANSWERS: 1. Bluto (John Belushi in *Animal House*), **2.** Boston (during the Boston Marathon), **3.** Pia Zadora, **4.** Gort, **5.** Marlon Brando (refusing Best Actor for *The Godfather*)

Do You Know **MATCHING QUIZ**?

Take 10 points for each correct answer. Maximum this page: 50 points!

MATCH the regular lines with the early TV characters who owned them:

1. "Hey there, Ralphie-Boy!"

a. Vern Albright

2. "Aw, turn blue!"

b. Kathy Anderson

3. "I don't mess around, boy!"

c. Arthur Fonzarelli

4. "Well—heh, heh—that's My Little Margie."

d. Ricky Nelson

5. "Ayyyyy!"

e. Ed Norton

ANSWERS: 1. e (*The Honeymooners*), **2.** b (*Father Knows Best*), **3.** d (*The Adventures of Ozzie and Harriet*), **4.** a (*My Little Margie*), **5.** c (*Happy Days*)

Do You Know **AD SLOGANS**?

Take 10 points for each correct answer. Maximum this page: 50 points!

MATCH the memorable lines with the products:

1. "Mother, *please*—I'd rather do it myself!"   **a.** Ban

2. "Sorry, Charlie!"   **b.** StarKist

3. "Bet you can't eat just one!"   **c.** Alka-Seltzer

4. "I can't believe I ate the whole thing!"   **d.** Lay's

5. "Takes the worry out of being close"   **e.** Anacin

SCORE FOR THIS TEST: _____ TOTAL SO FAR: _____

Do You Know **WHO**?

Take 4 points for each correct answer. Maximum this page: 20 points!

1. WHO wrote the famous reply to the little girl, telling her: "Yes, Virginia, there is a Santa Claus"?

    a. A teacher
    b. A newspaper editor
    c. A president of the United States
    d. The little girl's grandmother

2. WHO first said on film "The dingo's got my baby!"?

    a. Paul Hogan
    b. Olivia Newton-John
    c. Cher
    d. Meryl Streep

3. WHO created "Keep on Truckin'" and Fritz the Cat?

    a. R. Crumb
    b. Charles M. Schulz
    c. Felix T. Leon
    d. S. Hurok

4. WHO was known as The Old Perfesser?

    a. Yogi Berra
    b. Casey Stengel
    c. Albert Einstein
    d. Andy Rooney

5. WHO played Big Daddy in *Cat on a Hot Tin Roof?*

    a. Raymond Burr
    b. William Conrad
    c. Burl Ives
    d. Victor Buono

SCORE FOR THIS TEST: _____ TOTAL SO FAR: _____

ANSWERS: 1. b (Francis P. Church, in the *New York Sun*), **2.** d (in *A Cry in the Dark*), **3.** a, **4.** b, **5.** c

Do You Know **FILL-IN QUIZ**?

Take 10 points for each correct answer. Maximum this page: 50 points!

1. Had to give back her Pulitzer Prize after it came out that she had faked her big story: _____ _____.

2. What George Jessel, Bob Newhart, Shelley Berman, and Lily Tomlin had in common: _____.

3. Pleaded for mercy because "Our mothers all are junkies, our fathers all are drunks": the _____.

4. Have kids named Bart, Lisa, and Maggie: _____ and _____ _____.

5. Batman and The Incredible Hulk have this given name in common: _____.

SCORE FOR THIS TEST: _____ TOTAL SO FAR: _____

ANSWERS: 1. Janet Cooke, no longer of the *Washington Post*, **2.** telephone (George, Bob, and Shelley delivered mock phone call monologues, Lily played Ernestine the operator), **3.** the Jets in *West Side Story*, **4.** Homer and Marge Simpson (in *The Simpsons*), **5.** Bruce (Batman's secret identity is Bruce Wayne, Hulk's is Bruce Banner)

Do You Know **WHAT**?

Take 10 points for each correct answer. Maximum this page: 50 points!

1. WHAT comes in many varieties, among them box, finish, and common?
- a. Fruit preserves
- b. Olive oil
- c. Nails
- d. Earthworms

2. In *The Graduate,* Benjamin drives a red sports car. WHAT kind?
- a. Mercedes 190SL
- b. Alfa Romeo Spider
- c. Triumph Spitfire
- d. Sunbeam Alpine

3. WHAT music was played as wrestling legend Gorgeous George and his valet entered the ring?
- a. "Anything You Can Do I Can Do Better"
- b. "Here Comes the Bride"
- c. "I'll be Seeing You"
- d. "Pomp and Circumstance"

4. WHAT was Dennis the Menace's family name?
- a. Benes
- b. Ketchum
- c. Wilson
- d. Mitchell

5. Simon and Garfunkel originally sang under WHAT name?
- a. Paul and Art
- b. Garfunkel and Simon
- c. Tom and Jerry
- d. The Queens Boys

SCORE FOR THIS TEST: _____ TOTAL SO FAR: _____

Do You Know **HOW MANY**?

Take 2 points for each correct answer. Maximum this page: 10 points!

1. HOW MANY numbered squares on a Bingo card?

    a. 24
    b. 25
    c. 36
    d. 75

2. HOW MANY herbs and spices does KFC say flavor their chicken recipe?

    a. 3
    b. 8
    c. 11
    d. 44

3. In his record-setting string of appearances on *Jeopardy,* about HOW MANY bucks did Ken Jennings win?

    a. 1 million
    b. 3 million
    c. 5 million
    d. 6 million

4. In *The Pajama Game,* HOW MANY more cents did the workers want every hour, even though it "doesn't buy a helluva lot"?

    a. 5
    b. 7
    c. 7.5
    d. 11

5. Joe Mankiewicz's *Cleopatra,* starring Elizabeth Taylor and Richard Burton, was a long movie. Just HOW MANY minutes long was it?

    a. 159
    b. 243
    c. 299
    d. 343

      SCORE FOR THIS TEST: _____ TOTAL SO FAR: _____

ANSWERS: 1. a, **2.** c, **3.** c, **4.** c ("but give it to me every hour, 40 hours every week"), **5.** b

Do You Know **NAMES**?

Take 10 points for each correct answer. Maximum this page: 50 points!

Pair the celebrities on the left with the pre-showbiz **NAMES** on the right:

1. Tammy Wynette

a. Anna Mae Bullock

2. Patsy Cline

b. Virginia Patterson Hensley

3. Judy Garland

c. Virginia Pugh

4. Tina Turner

d. Arnold Dorsey

5. Englebert Humperdink

e. Frances Gumm

SCORE FOR THIS TEST: _____ TOTAL SO FAR: _____

Do You Know **IN COMMON**?

Take 10 points for each correct answer. Maximum this page: 50 points!

1. What do Maldon, England and the Guérande Peninsula in Brittany, France have IN COMMON?

2. What do Richard Raskind and Walter Carlos have IN COMMON?

3. What do Melbourne Park and Roland Garros have IN COMMON?

4. What do José Feliciano and Rosanne Barr have IN COMMON?

5. What do Bub O'Casey and Fred Mertz have IN COMMON?

SCORE FOR THIS TEST: _____ TOTAL SO FAR: _____

Do You Know **WHO**?

Take 10 points for each correct answer. Maximum this page: 50 points!

1. WHO was Chatsworth Osborne Jr.?
   a. Character on TV's *The Many Loves of Dobie Gillis*
   b. Vice president of the United States under Warren G. Harding
   c. Director of many movie Westerns
   d. Bass in the rock group Maynard and the Krebs

2. WHO holds the record for most home runs in a World Series (five)?
   a. Lou Gehrig
   b. Barry Bonds
   c. Lenny Dykstra
   d. Reggie Jackson

3. WHO was Henry Morton Stanley, who tracked and found Dr. Livingstone?
   a. A missionary
   b. A reporter
   c. An animal trainer
   d. A British government official

4. WHO said that Leonard Bernstein "uses music as an accompaniment to his conducting"?
   a. Jack Paar
   b. Frank Sinatra
   c. Oscar Levant
   d. Madonna

5. In *The Empire Strikes Back*, Darth Vader famously told Luke Skywalker "I am your father." WHO was the voice of Vader?
   a. James Earl Jones
   b. Orson Welles
   c. Jon "Bowzer" Bauman
   d. Lorenzo Music

SCORE FOR THIS TEST: _____ TOTAL SO FAR: _____

ANSWERS: 1. a (an annoying rich kid), **2.** d, **3.** b (for the *New York Herald*), **4.** c, **5.** a

Do You Know **WHAT'S WHERE**?

Take 10 points for each correct answer. Maximum this page: 50 points!

Match the neighborhoods and the cities:

1. Georgetown

a. Los Angeles

2. Yaletown

b. Marrakesh

3. Plaka

c. Vancouver

4. Medina

d. Washington, D.C.

5. Westlake

e. Athens

SCORE FOR THIS TEST: _____ TOTAL SO FAR: _____

Do You Know **WHAT**?

Take 4 points for each correct answer. Maximum this page: 20 points!

1. WHAT was the title of the 1928 Disney cartoon that made Mickey Mouse famous?
- a. *Steamboat Willie*
- b. *Steamboat Mickey*
- c. *Mickey Loves Minnie*
- d. *Eek! A Mouse!*

2. The city of Britt, Iowa hosts an annual festival celebrating WHAT?
- a. Frisbees
- b. Tomatoes
- c. Hoboes
- d. Rock 'n' Roll

3. Humorist Roger Price's series of super-quick cartoons with captions like "A Ship Arriving Too Late to Save a Drowning Witch," "Tower of Pisa As Seen By Leaning Tourist," and "Man Playing Trombone in Phone Booth" were called WHAT?
- a. Cartooties
- b. Cartoodles
- c. Droodles
- d. Snappers

4. A sign in a French filling station that reads "7j/7" concerns WHAT?
- a. Octane
- b. Opening days
- c. Repair services offered
- d. Newspapers for sale

5. In *Fiddler On the Roof,* Golde sings to her husband, Tevye: "Do you love me?" WHAT's Tevye's first response?
- a. "Do I *what?*"
- b. "Of course, dear."
- c. "I suppose I do."
- d. "Sure thing—what's for supper?"

SCORE FOR THIS TEST: _____ TOTAL SO FAR: _____

Do You Know **AIRLINES**?

Take 10 points for each correct answer. Maximum this page: 50 points!

Match the airlines and their hub cities:

1. Aer Lingus

a. Amsterdam

2. KLM

b. Hong Kong

3. Dragonair

c. Madrid

4. Jat

d. Dublin and Cork

5. Iberia

e. Belgrade

SCORE FOR THIS TEST: _____ TOTAL SO FAR: _____

Do You Know **WHO**?

Take 4 points for each correct answer. Maximum this page: 20 points!

1. WHO was the inspiration for Billy Crystal's *Saturday Night Live* character Fernando, famous for the catchphrase "You look maahhhvelous!"?

   a. Sammy Davis Jr.
   b. Fernando Lamas
   c. Ricardo Montalban
   d. Crystal's uncle Fred

2. WHO was the other face on Elton John's several "Face to Face" tours?

   a. Sting
   b. Billy Joel
   c. Rob Thomas
   d. Rod Stewart

3. WHO is the father of jazz singer Norah Jones, also a music maker?

   a. Tiny Tim
   b. Philly Joe Jones
   c. Julian Bream
   d. Ravi Shankar

4. WHO created the character Fagin, who lived off the money stolen by children under his tutelage?

   a. William Shakespeare
   b. Rod Serling
   c. Charles Dickens
   d. Jane Austen

5. WHO was Dr. Winston O'Boogie?

   a. Surgeon general of the U.S. under Nixon
   b. A pseudonym of John Lennon
   c. A character in *Doonesbury*
   d. Music writing partner of Eubie Blake

SCORE FOR THIS TEST: _____ TOTAL SO FAR: _____

Do You Know **FILL-IN QUIZ**?

Take 10 points for each correct answer. Maximum this page: 50 points!

1. E.T.'s favorite food: _____ _____.

2. Dan Quayle's first name is James. His middle name, from which he derived "Dan," is _____.

3. Minnie Pearl wore a straw hat with artificial flowers and a _____ _____.

4. *Old Mother Hubbard went to the cupboard*
To get her poor daughter a dress.
When she got there, her cupboard was bare,

_____ _____ _____ _____ _____ _____ _____.

5. Doogie Howser's best friend, Vinnie Delpino, got into Doogie's room to visit by climbing _____ _____ _____.

SCORE FOR THIS TEST: _____ TOTAL SO FAR: _____

Do You Know **ANALOGIES**?

Take 10 points for each correct answer. Maximum this page: 50 points!

1. Walter Matthau is to Jack Klugman as Jack Lemmon is to _____

2. Constantinople is to Istanbul as Upper Volta is to _____

3. Köchel is to Mozart as Deutsch is to _____

4. The Owl and the Pussycat are to a beautiful pea-green boat as Wynken, Blynken, and Nod are to _____

5. *Phantom of the Paradise* is to Brian De Palma as *The Birds* is to _____

SCORE FOR THIS TEST: _____ TOTAL SO FAR: _____

ANSWERS: 1. Tony Randall (*The Odd Couple's* Oscar and Felix, movie and TV versions), **2.** Burkina Faso (new names for old), **3.** Schubert (cataloguers of composers' works), **4.** a tub ("Rub-a-Dub-Dub"), **5.** Alfred Hitchcock (director)

Do You Know **CATCHPHRASES**?

Take 4 points for each correct answer. Maximum this page: 20 points!

1. "Well, ex*cu-u-use* me!"

a. George Gobel

2. "Is that your final answer?"

b. Jackie Gleason

3. "Hey, Vern!"

c. Steve Martin

4. "Well, I'll be a dirty bird!"

d. Ernest P. Worrell

5. "Well, har, har, hardy-har har!"

e. Regis Philbin

SCORE FOR THIS TEST: _____ TOTAL SO FAR: _____

Do You Know **CB SLANG**?

Take 4 points for each correct answer. Maximum this page: 20 points!

Match the CB radio terms with their definitions:

1. Smokey

a. pay a fine

2. Handle

b. state cop

3. Cash register

c. message received

4. Feed the bears

d. nickname

5. 10-4

e. tollbooth

SCORE FOR THIS TEST: _____ TOTAL SO FAR: _____

Do You Know **FILL-IN QUIZ**?

Take 10 points for each correct answer. Maximum this page: 50 points!

1. A Swing Era trumpeter, a nineteenth-century outlaw, and an NBA star have the same last name: _____.

2. "Are you smoking more now _____ _____ _____ _____?"

3. *Streetcar* line: "I have always depended upon _____ _____ _____ _____."

4. Richie Petrie's middle name and a famous sled: _____.

5. "Two all-beef patties, _____ _____ _____ _____ _____ _____ _____ _____ _____ _____."

SCORE FOR THIS TEST: _____ TOTAL SO FAR: _____

Do You Know **TRUE OR FALSE**?

Take 4 points for each correct answer. Maximum this page: 20 points!

1. Among the famous folk who have appeared on the soap opera *One Life to Live* are Hugh Downs, Sammy Davis Jr., Reba McEntire, Little Richard, and Dr. Ruth.
_____ True   _____ False

2. Before he became a teen singing idol, Frankie Avalon was an acclaimed trumpet player.
_____ True   _____ False

3. Jackie Gleason once hosted a television game show. Its first weekly installment was so bad that he spent the entire second show apologizing. The third week, he changed to a safer format: a talk show.
_____ True   _____ False

4. Howard Hughes built a gigantic airplane, the *Spruce Goose,* so called because to conserve metal in wartime the craft was made chiefly of spruce wood.
_____ True   _____ False

5. One of Woody Allen's early writing jobs was for *Candid Camera.*
_____ True   _____ False

SCORE FOR THIS TEST: _____   TOTAL SO FAR: _____

Do You Know **WHO**?

Take 10 points for each correct answer. Maximum this page: 50 points!

1. WHO shot and killed Indian prime minister Indira Gandhi, in 1984?
   a. An unidentified gunman who cursed her in Russian
   b. Two of her bodyguards
   c. A woman who had just shaken her hand in a receiving line
   d. A sniper who was never found

2. In 1938, an art collector discovered some paintings in the window of a drug-store in Hoosick Falls, New York, and soon the whole world knew about the artist. WHO became internationally famous and had a career for decades thanks to this lucky find?
   a. Grandma Moses
   b. Andy Warhol
   c. Georgia O'Keeffe
   d. Robert Rauschenberg

3. WHO first published the tale of *Goldilocks and the Three Bears?*
   a. The Grimm brothers
   b. Robert Southey
   c. Dr. Seuss
   d. Hans Christian Anderson

4. In Kay Starr's hit song, WHO danced "The Rock and Roll Waltz"?
   a. Mom and Dad
   b. Ted and I
   c. Everyone
   d. All the hepcats

5. WHO managed Elvis?
   a. Sam Phillips
   b. Brian Epstein
   c. Colonel Tom Parker
   d. Carl Perkins

SCORE FOR THIS TEST: _____ TOTAL SO FAR: _____

Do You Know **WHAT**?

Take 10 points for each correct answer. Maximum this page: 50 points!

1. WHAT city is named after a long-running television program?
- a. Dallas, Texas
- b. Truth or Consequences, New Mexico
- c. Tarzana, California
- d. Meet the Press, South Dakota

2. WHAT was the first name of Jack Paar's daughter, occasionally mentioned in his monologues?
- a. Alexandra
- b. Hermione
- c. Geneviève
- d. Randy

3. WHAT is Robert Trent Jones known for?
- a. Playing golf blindfolded
- b. Designing golf courses
- c. Hitting a grand slam in the 1982 baseball World Series
- d. Inventing Velcro

4. WHAT is crêpe de chine?
- a. A kind of silk
- b. A kind of paper
- c. A Szechuan pancake
- d. Fine but unpainted Irish porcelain

5. WHAT was Rommel's asparagus?
- a. A vegetable dish once popular in Germany, now known to be poisonous
- b. A wooden stake used by Nazis to damage invading gliders during WWII
- c. A wrestling hold outlawed in all 50 states
- d. A card game that uses three decks and an extra joker

SCORE FOR THIS TEST: _____ TOTAL SO FAR: _____

Do You Know **WHEN**?

Take 10 points for each correct answer. Maximum this page: 50 points!

1. OK, you know that Gatorade was developed for the football team at the University of Florida. But WHEN?

    a. 1936
    b. 1965
    c. 1972
    d. 1975

2. And WHEN were the first boxes of Crayolas sold?

    a. 1803
    b. 1864
    c. 1903
    d. 1960

3. WHEN did the volcano Vesuvius erupt, destroying Pompeii and Herculaneum?

    a. About 200 BC
    b. 79 BC
    c. AD 79
    d. AD 355

4. WHEN was "A Black and White Night," the brilliant all-star concert honoring and featuring Roy Orbison, first aired on television?

    a. January 3, 1964
    b. January 3, 1970
    c. January 3, 1980
    d. January 3, 1988

5. WHEN was Prozac approved for use in the USA?

    a. 1948
    b. 1968
    c. 1987
    d. 1993

SCORE FOR THIS TEST: _____ TOTAL SO FAR: _____

ANSWERS: 1. b, 2. c, 3. b, 4. d, 5. c

Do You Know **WHERE**?

Take 10 points for each correct answer. Maximum this page: 50 points!

1. WHERE did Americans pick up the catchphrases "Sorry about that, Chief" and "Would you believe . . . ?"
- a. The movie *Airplane*
- b. The spy-spoof TV series *Get Smart*
- c. Vice President George H.W. Bush
- d. *Batman* comics and the TV show

2. WHERE does the name Pokémon come from?
- a. A contraction of *Poketto Monsutâ* (Pocket Monsters)
- b. The inventor's name, jumbled
- c. The inventor's mother's name, <u>un</u>jumbled
- d. A randomized naming program

3. In the song "American Pie," WHERE did the three men Don McLean admires more than any others take the last train?
- a. To Woodstock
- b. To Philly
- c. To the coast
- d. To Nowheresville

4. WHERE does the famous *Star Wars* bar scene take place?
- a. Doaba Guerfel, on the planet Corellia
- b. The space port city of Mos Eisley, on the planet Tatooine
- c. Bestine, called the capital of Tatooine
- d. It's never specified

5. In the Howard Hawks film *Red River,* WHERE in Texas does the showdown between John Wayne and Montgomery Clift take place?
- a. Austin
- b. Abilene
- c. Crawford
- d. Never stated

SCORE FOR THIS TEST: _____ TOTAL SO FAR: _____

Do You Know **WHY**?

Take 10 points for each correct answer. Maximum this page: 50 points!

1. WHY did Frank Zamboni invent the ice resurfacing machine that bears his name?

    a. On request of an NHL team

    b. To maintain the rink he and relatives operated in Southern California

    c. To prove to his father-in-law that he could do something big

    d. To win a bet

2. WHY did 11-year-old Samantha Smith go to Moscow?

    a. To prepare for the Winter Olympics in Sarajevo

    b. To play in the Tchaikovsky Piano Competition

    c. To compete in the first-ever English-Russian Spelling Bee

    d. Soviet leader Yuri Andropov invited her

3. After 27 years, service on the supersonic Concorde stopped. WHY?

    a. Environmental groups staged repeated protests

    b. Government support was discontinued

    c. Passengers declined and maintenance costs rose

    d. The fleet was aging and plans for building a new Concorde had been lost

4. WHY is green tea called that?

    a. It's made from only green leaves

    b. It's made from only young leaves

    c. It's made from unfermented leaves

    d. It's made by tea blenders in their first year on the job

5. The Queen of England celebrates her birthday twice each year: her actual birthday and an "official birthday" on a Saturday in June. WHY?

    a. To improve the chances of good weather for the official birthday parade

    b. The June date is a cover because no one knows her actual birth date for sure

    c. The June date is actually Queen Victoria's birthday, which by decree is to be celebrated by every future monarch

    d. The June date is actually the birthday of her father, King George VI, and every queen must celebrate the birthday of her father, to whom she owes the crown

SCORE FOR THIS TEST: _____ TOTAL SO FAR: _____

Do You Know **HOW**?

Take 10 points for each correct answer. Maximum this page: 50 points!

1. HOW did Watergate convict and radio host G. Gordon Liddy say he overcame his fear of rodents?

    a. He kept live mice in his sock drawer

    b. He roasted and ate a rat

    c. He wore Mickey Mouse ears, mouse whiskers, and a mouse tail every day for a month

    d. He stared in the mirror for hours on end, repeating "I am bigger, stronger, and smarter than any rodent on this good planet Earth"

2. HOW do basenjis differ from most other dogs?

    a. They don't bark

    b. They love to swim the backstroke

    c. They're swaybacked

    d. They can see around corners

3. HOW do ostriches differ from other birds?

    a. They don't make a sound

    b. The females don't lay eggs

    c. They have only two—not three or four—toes per foot

    d. None of the above

4. In *Moby Dick*, HOW does Ishmael survive in the water before he's rescued?

    a. By treading water

    b. By sitting on an islet until the *Rachel* comes along and saves him

    c. By floating on a makeshift raft he fastens from timbers stripped from the *Pequod*

    d. By hanging onto Queequeg's coffin

5. In *It Happened One Night*, HOW did Claudette Colbert and Clark Gable meet?

    a. They were introduced by their dentist

    b. They met at a church function

    c. They were on the same bus

    d. They were both finalists in a Trivia contest

SCORE FOR THIS TEST: _____ TOTAL SO FAR: _____

Do You Know **HOW MANY**?

Take 10 points for each correct answer. Maximum this page: 50 points!

1. HOW MANY years does it take to produce a cultivated pearl?

    a. 1–2
    b. 3–6
    c. 7–10
    d. more than 40

2. HOW MANY black keys on a standard piano keyboard?

    a. 36
    b. 46
    c. 52
    d. 88

3. HOW MANY stocks are followed in the Dow Jones Industrial Average?

    a. 30
    b. 130
    c. 330
    d. 3333

4. HOW MANY Earth days in a year on Venus?

    a. 29
    b. 225
    c. 365
    d. 666

5. In 1961, the USSR beat the USA into space. By HOW MANY days?

    a. 1
    b. 3
    c. 23
    d. 223

SCORE FOR THIS TEST: _____ TOTAL SO FAR: _____

ANSWERS: 1. b, **2.** a, **3.** a, **4.** b, **5.** c (from April 12 to May 5)

Do You Know **FILL-IN QUIZ?**

Take 10 points for each correct answer. Maximum this page: 50 points!

1. "Well you kissed me and stopped me from shaking. I need you today, oh _____."

2. Where Dr. Seuss saw it: _____ _____.

3. "_____ candles make a lovely light . . ."

4. She was "always window shopping but never stopping to buy": _____ _____.

5. Baseball Hall of Famer _____ _____ was known as "Double X."

SCORE FOR THIS TEST: _____ **TOTAL SO FAR:** _____

Do You Know **WHAT**?

Take 4 points for each correct answer. Maximum this page: 20 points!

1. WHAT does "just thinking about tomorrow" do for Annie?
- a. "Makes a girl feel happy, and believe me, sad's no fun"
- b. "Clears away the cobwebs and the sorrow till there's none"
- c. "That's the way that you can put your blues all on the run"
- d. "Lifts a burden from your shoulders that can weigh a ton"

3. WHAT were the words spoken by Thomas Edison, in 1877, when he made the first recording of the human voice?
- a. "Mary had a little lamb"
- b. "Mr. Watson, come here, I need you"
- c. "One, two, three, four"
- d. "I think this thing is working"

2. WHAT does the acronym LASER stand for?
- a. Light Accelerated by Severely Enhanced Radiation
- b. Loosely Applied Stressed Energy, Recovered
- c. Light Amplification by Stimulated Emission of Radiation
- d. Leveled, Augmented and Striated Energy Resource

4. The BBC, the Beeb, the world's largest radio and television outfit— WHAT do the initials mean?
- a. British Broadcasting Company
- b. British Broadcasting Corporation
- c. Broadcasts from Britain Consolidated
- d. Big Broadcast Company

5. "You'd better tell the captain we've got to land as soon as we can. This woman has to be gotten to a hospital." "A hospital? What is it?" "It's a big building with patients, but that's not important right now." This dialogue could only come from WHAT movie?
- a. *Duck Soup*
- b. *Airplane!*
- c. *Blazing Saddles*
- d. *Wayne's World*

SCORE FOR THIS TEST: _____ TOTAL SO FAR: _____

Do You Know **WHICH**?

Take 4 points for each correct answer. Maximum this page: 20 points!

1. Koo Stark, a softcore porn actress, was romantically linked with WHICH bold-face name?
   a. Burt Reynolds
   b. Kim Jong Il
   c. Prince Andrew
   d. Rosie O'Donnell

2. In WHICH of his many enduring hit songs did Johnny Mathis say he was "as helpless as a kitten up a tree"?
   a. "Chances Are"
   b. "Misty"
   c. "It's Not For Me to Say"
   d. "A Certain Smile"

3. On her first show of 2004, Oprah Winfrey gave a new Pontiac to all 276 members of her studio audience. (Or, to be more precise, Pontiac did.) But WHICH earlier megastar was noted for giving Cadillacs to friends, relatives, and strangers?
   a. Elvis Presley
   b. Bob Hope
   c. Johnny Carson
   d. Phil Donahue

4. WHICH bird has been clocked diving from on high in the neighborhood of 200 mph?
   a. Barn owl
   b. Cooper's hawk
   c. Black-throated diver
   d. Peregrine falcon

5. On WHICH television series did Tom Poston regularly appear?
   a. *The Steve Allen Show*
   b. *To Tell the Truth*
   c. *Mork and Mindy*
   d. *Newhart*
   e. all of the above

SCORE FOR THIS TEST: _____ TOTAL SO FAR: _____

ANSWERS: 1. c, 2. b, 3. a, 4. d, 5. e

Do You Know **WHICH—ODD ONE OUT**?

Take 4 points for each correct answer. Maximum this page: 20 points!

1. WHICH actress has *never* played Cleopatra on the big screen?

    a. Cher
    b. Elizabeth Taylor
    c. Vivian Leigh
    d. Claudette Colbert

2. WHICH line *isn't* from the Bible?

    a. "There is no new thing under the sun."
    b. "To eat, and to drink, and to be merry."
    c. "We are such stuff as dreams are made on,
       and our little life is rounded with a sleep."
    d. "Vanity of vanities . . . all is vanity."

3. WHICH character *didn't* Mel Blanc provide the voice for?

    a. Daffy Duck
    b. Porky Pig
    c. Barney Rubble
    d. Minnie Mouse

4. He wasn't only Ralph Kramden: Jackie Gleason played a lot of other roles, on television and in the movies. WHICH did he *never* play?

    a. The Poor Soul
    b. Minnesota Fats
    c. Joe the Bartender
    d. Mr. Saturday Night

5. WHICH after-dark comment was *never* uttered on *The Waltons?*

    a. "Good night, John-Boy."
    b. "Good night, Mary Ellen."
    c. "Good night, Jason."
    d. "Good night, Erin."
    e. "Good night, Earl."
    f. ."Good night, Ben."
    g. "Good night, Jim-Bob."
    h. "Good night, Elizabeth."

SCORE FOR THIS TEST: _____ TOTAL SO FAR: _____

Do You Know **FILL-IN QUIZ?**

Take 10 points for each correct answer. Maximum this page: 50 points!

1. *Even a man who is pure in heart*
And says his prayers by night
May become a wolf when the wolfbane blooms
And _____ _____ _____ _____ _____.

2. Jell-O: "America's most _____ dessert."

3. Malvina Reynolds lyric: "Little boxes on the hillside, little boxes made of _____ - _____."

4. Dick and Jane's dog and cat: _____ and _____.

5. "Say goodnight, Dick." "_____ _____."

SCORE FOR THIS TEST: _____ TOTAL SO FAR: _____

ANSWERS: 1. the autumn moon is bright (*The Wolf Man*; in sequels it was "the moon is full and bright"), **2.** famous, **3.** ticky-tacky, **4.** Spot, Puff, **5.** "Goodnight, Dick" (*Rowan & Martin's Laugh-In*)

Do You Know **WHO**?

Take 4 points for each correct answer. Maximum this page: 20 points!

1. Sure, you know that Michael Jackson was the youngest of The Jackson Five. We'll give you brother Jermaine. Now, of these four, WHO were the other three?

    a. Jackie
    b. Tito
    c. LaToya
    d. Marlon

2. WHO's the principal of Riverdale High School, attended by Archie, Jughead, Betty, Veronica, and their assorted pals and rivals?

    a. Miss Grundy
    b. Mr. Weatherbee
    c. Mr. Cleats
    d. Dr. Copeland

3. WHO, early in his life, was known as Samuel Goldfish?

    a. Movie mogul Sam Goldwyn (as in Metro-Goldwyn-Mayer, MGM)
    b. U.S. Senator and presidential candidate Barry Goldwater
    c. Underwater explorer Jacques Cousteau
    d. Clinton-era national security advisor Sandy Berger

4. WHO was Ezra H. Fitch?

    a. U.S. Navy admiral
    b. Settler of Fitchburg, Massachusetts
    c. Former NBA coach
    d. Partner of David T. Abercrombie

5. Of these four people named Simon, WHO's the oldest?

    a. Paul Simon
    b. Carly Simon
    c. Neil Simon
    d. Simon Rattle

SCORE FOR THIS TEST: _____ TOTAL SO FAR: _____

ANSWERS: 1. all but c, 2. b, 3. a, 4. d, 5. c

Do You Know **IN COMMON**?

Take 20 points for each correct answer. Maximum this page: 100 points!

1. What do Eartha Kitt, Buffy Sainte-Marie, Wayne Newton, and Tina Turner have IN COMMON?

2. What do a Texas stripper and the founder of Mothers Against Drunk Drivers have IN COMMON?

3. What do Blondie and Dagwood Bumstead, Wally Amos, and your computer have IN COMMON?

4. What do Floyd R. Turbo and Emily Litella have IN COMMON?

5. What do Ethel Merman, Angela Lansbury, Tyne Daly, Bette Midler, and Betty Buckley have IN COMMON?

SCORE FOR THIS TEST: _____ TOTAL SO FAR: _____

Do You Know **CAMPAIGN SLOGANS**?

Take 10 points for each correct answer. Maximum this page: 50 points!

Match the slogans with the Presidential candidates:

1. "In your heart you know he's right"

a. Clinton

2. "Come home, America"

b. McGovern

3. "It's time to change America"

c. Goldwater

4. "Go clean for Gene"

d. Reagan

5. "Are you better off than you were
four years ago?"

e. McCarthy

SCORE FOR THIS TEST: _____ TOTAL SO FAR: _____

Do You Know **WHAT**?

Take 4 points for each correct answer. Maximum this page: 20 points!

1. American International Standard, Hesitation, and Viennese are styles of WHAT?

    a. Tableware
    b. Dumpling
    c. Truck Engine
    d. Waltz

2. A garden with soil pH of 4.5 needs WHAT for balance?

    a. Something alkaline, like ground limestone or ash
    b. Something acid, like gypsum or ground sulfur
    c. Sand
    d. Compost

3. The Spencer Method and the Palmer Method—methods of WHAT?

    a. Guitar playing
    b. Typing
    c. Penmanship
    d. Bridge

4. The early reality TV show *An American Family* chronicled the messy lives of WHAT family?

    a. The Lords
    b. The Leeds
    c. The Louds
    d. The Lunds

5. In *Bringing Up Baby,* WHAT song do Katharine Hepburn and Cary Grant sing to a leopard?

    a. "Good Night, Irene"
    b. "I Love You Truly"
    c. "The Girl That I Marry"
    d. "I Can't Give You Anything But Love"

SCORE FOR THIS TEST: _____ TOTAL SO FAR: _____

ANSWERS: 1. d, 2. a, 3. c, 4. c, 5. d

Do You Know **MOVIE ENDINGS**?

Take 10 points for each correct answer. Maximum this page: 50 points!

Match the last lines of dialogue with the classic motion pictures:

1. "I never had any friends later on like the ones I had when I was twelve. Jesus, does anyone?"

a. *Gone with the Wind*

2. "After all, tomorrow is another day."

b. *A Day at the Races*

3. "I really am a horse doctor, but marry me and I'll never look at another horse."

c. *A Star Is Born*

4. "Where ya headed, cowboy?"
"Nowhere special." "Nowhere special. I always wanted to go there." "Come on."

d. *Stand By Me*

5. "Hello, everybody. This is Mrs. Norman Maine."

e. *Blazing Saddles*

SCORE FOR THIS TEST: _____ TOTAL SO FAR: _____

Do You Know **MOVIE ENDINGS**?

Take 10 points for each correct answer. Maximum this page: 50 points!

More last lines from the big screen:

1. "I was cured, all right."

a. *Annie Hall*

2. "This was the story of Howard Beale, the first known instance of a man who was killed because he had lousy ratings."

b. *A Clockwork Orange*

3. "And we'll go on forever, Pa . . . 'cause we're the people."

c. *Back to the Future*

4. " . . . most of us need the eggs."

d. *The Grapes of Wrath*

5. "Roads? Where we're going we don't need roads."

e. *Network*

SCORE FOR THIS TEST: _____ TOTAL SO FAR: _____

ANSWERS: 1. b, 2. e, 3. d, 4. a, 5. c

Do You Know **FILL-IN QUIZ**?

Take 10 points for each correct answer. Maximum this page: 50 points!

1. Cagney line: "Look, Ma, _____ _____ _____ _____!"

2. Alter ego of John Clayton, Lord Greystoke: _____.

3. "Thank Heaven for Little Girls" movie: _____.

4. Richard Simmons video series: *Sweatin'* _____ _____ _____.

5. Defensive lineman Rosey Grier's surprising hobbies: _____ and _____.

SCORE FOR THIS TEST: _____ TOTAL SO FAR: _____

ANSWERS: 1. top of the world (*White Heat*), **2.** Tarzan, **3.** *Gigi*, **4.** *to the Oldies*, **5.** needlepoint and macrame

Do You Know **WHY**?

Take 20 points for each correct answer. Maximum this page: 100 points!

1. WHY is the hand-held wireless device called a BlackBerry?

    a. It was named for the inventor, Charles Strawson Blackberry

    b. It was named for the company's chief backer, Robert Blackberry Christofede

    c. Blackberry is the favorite ice cream flavor of the company's chief engineer

    d. A consultant said the buttons look like strawberry seeds; it was just a step or two to the final name

2. WHY are flamingos pink?

    a. They eat brine shrimp, which dine on algae rich in carotene, which makes their feathers pink

    b. They have glands that excrete a pinkish fluid that covers their entire bodies

    c. The sun affects their pigment; flamingos kept indoors are a pale yellow

    d. Zoologists have never been able to isolate the cause

3. WHY is caviar usually served with a spreader made of mother of pearl, wood, gold, horn, or even plastic—something other than silver or steel?

    a. That's what the tsar preferred

    b. Metal cools the caviar excessively

    c. Metal interacts with the roe and makes it smell like onion

    d. Some believe metal affects the taste

4. WHY did Johann Sebastian Bach, at age 20, walk from Arnstadt to Lübeck, some 250 miles?

    a. To lose weight

    b. To study with Pachelbel

    c. To conduct the premiere of his *Brandenburg Concerto No. 1*

    d. To hear Buxtehude play organ

5. WHY is country songwriter and singer Bill Anderson called "Whisperin' Bill?"

    a. He sings very gently

    b. He had a habit of whispering asides to his singing partners during a performance

    c. He had a habit of muttering to himself while he soloed on guitar

    d. He was totally mute for the first twenty years of his life

    SCORE FOR THIS TEST: _____ TOTAL SO FAR: _____

Do You Know **WHAT**?

Take 10 points for each correct answer. Maximum this page: 50 points!

1. WHAT is the best way to describe a manatee's tail?
- a. Arrow-shaped
- b. Paddle-shaped
- c. Forked
- d. Non-existent

2. Comedian Joan Rivers and cartoonist Charles Schulz may not have had much in common in their ideas about humor, but each had a dog named WHAT?
- a. Spike
- b. Snoopy
- c. Linus
- d. Fang

3. WHAT was Flipper?
- a. A faithful dog
- b. An intelligent dolphin
- c. A drunk monkey
- d. A circus seal

4. In the 1931 movie, WHAT did Count Dracula call wolves?
- a. "My little canine companions"
- b. "Everybody's friend, nobody's enemy"
- c. "Children of the night"
- d. "The most glorious creatures in nature's world"

5. Alpine, Boer, Nubian, and Pygmy are breeds of WHAT?
- a. Parrot
- b. Cow
- c. Goat
- d. Pony

SCORE FOR THIS TEST: _____ TOTAL SO FAR: _____

ANSWERS: 1. b, 2. d, 3. b, 4. c, 5. c

Do You Know **FILL-IN QUIZ**?

Take 10 points for each correct answer. Maximum this page: 50 points!

1. Two sets of Bobbsey Twins: _____ and _____ (the older pair), _____ and _____ (the younger).

2. Diana, Mary, and Florence (later Cindy): The _____.

3. "One hen. One hen, two ducks. One hen, two ducks, _____ _____ _____."

4. "Light she was, and like a fairy, and her shoes were _____ _____."

5. "The stockings were hung by the chimney _____ _____."

SCORE FOR THIS TEST: _____ TOTAL SO FAR: _____

ANSWERS: 1. Bert & Nan, Freddie & Flossie, **2.** Supremes, **3.** three squawking geese (and it goes on . . . thanks, Jerry Lewis), **4.** number nine ("Oh My Darling, Clementine"), **5.** with care ("A Visit From St. Nicholas")

Do You Know **WHAT**?

Take 20 points for each correct answer. Maximum this page: 100 points!

1. WHAT's a cordwainer?
- a. A rope maker
- b. A shoemaker
- c. A kitchen assistant
- d. A choir director

2. WHAT was gambler and gunman Doc Holliday's day job?
- a. Surgeon
- b. Psychiatrist
- c. Pediatrician
- d. Dentist

3. WHAT kind of doctor was Benjamin Spock?
- a. Pediatrician
- b. Ear, nose, and throat specialist
- c. Homeopathic physician
- d. Veterinarian

4. WHAT kind of work was Diana Spencer doing while she dated Prince Charles?
- a. Cook in an Indian restaurant
- b. Graphic artist
- c. Fashion photographer's assistant
- d. Aide in a kindergarten

5. Close readers of *Peanuts* know Charlie Brown's father's occupation. So WHAT was he?
- a. A teacher
- b. A fireman
- c. A barber
- d. A standup comic

SCORE FOR THIS TEST: _____ TOTAL SO FAR: _____

ANSWERS: 1. b, 2. d, 3. a, 4. d, 5. c

Do You Know **WHEN**?

Take 20 points for each correct answer. Maximum this page: 100 points!

1. WHEN were these bears born? You don't have to know the years; just put them in chronological order, please.

    a. Smokey
    b. Yogi
    c. Pooh
    d. Teddy

2. A.J. Foyt was one of just three four-time winners of the Indy 500 since its start in 1911. WHEN was the last time he won?

    a. 1964
    b. 1967
    c. 1977
    d. 1988

3. Attention hobbit fans: WHEN were the three *Lord of the Rings* movies released:

    a. December 2001, December 2002, December 2003
    b. December 2000, December 2001, December 2002
    c. December 1999, December 2001, December 2003
    d. June 2000, December 2001, June 2003

4. WHEN do porcupines' quills get sharp?

    a. At birth
    b. A day or so after birth
    c. About age 1
    d. About age 3

5. As far as is known, just one example of the British Guiana one-cent magenta exists today. WHEN was that rare stamp issued?

    a. 1818
    b. 1856
    c. 1899
    d. 1900

SCORE FOR THIS TEST: _____ TOTAL SO FAR: _____

Do You Know **WHERE**?

Take 20 points for each correct answer. Maximum this page: 100 points!

1. WHERE does the main route of the Trans-Siberian Railway run?

    a. Leningrad to Vladivostok

    b. Minsk to Irkutsk

    c. Moscow to Petropavlovsk

    d. Moscow to Vladivostok

2. WHERE did the Lambada dance craze come from?

    a. Brazil

    b. Portugal

    c. South Carolina

    d. Scotland

3. WHERE would you find a malar bone?

    a. In your foot

    b. In your cheek

    c. Just below your knee

    d. Just above your coccyx

4. WHERE did the Civil War battle between the Union sloop USS *Kearsarge* and the rebel raider CSS *Alabama* take place?

    a. In the Gulf of Mexico

    b. Near Martha's Vineyard, Massachusetts

    c. Off the coast of Norfolk, Virginia

    d. Off the coast of Cherbourg, France

5. The Hang Seng index follows daily listings from WHERE?

    a. The Hong Kong Stock Exchange

    b. The Taiwan Stock Exchange

    c. The Singapore Exchange

    d. The Tokyo Stock Exchange

SCORE FOR THIS TEST: _____ TOTAL SO FAR: _____

ANSWERS: 1. d, 2. a, 3. b, 4. d, 5. a

Do You Know **MATCHING QUIZ**?

Take 10 points for each correct answer. Maximum this page: 50 points!

Match the notables with their former occupations:

1. William Faulkner

a. teacher

2. Lyndon B. Johnson

b. patent office clerk

3. Albert Einstein

c. Custom House employee

4. Sting

d. university postmaster

5. Nathaniel Hawthorne

e. teacher

SCORE FOR THIS TEST: _____ TOTAL SO FAR: _____

Do You Know **FILL-IN QUIZ**?

Take 10 points for each correct answer. Maximum this page: 50 points!

1. Frosty the Snowman had "a corncob pipe and a button nose and _____
_____ _____ _____ _____ _____."

2. "Your mission, Mr. Phelps, should you _____ _____ _____ _____ . . ."

3. "How much is that doggy in the window, the one with the _____ _____?"

4. Each of Disney's Three Little Pigs builds his house of a different material, and each plays a different musical instrument. The brick brother plays _____, the sticks brother plays _____, and the straw brother plays _____.

5. *Twelve Angry Men* tells about a jury deciding the fate of a young man accused of murdering _____ _____.

SCORE FOR THIS TEST: _____ **TOTAL SO FAR:** _____

ANSWERS: 1. two eyes made out of coal, **2.** choose to accept it (from the recorded instructions in the opening scene of each episode of the *Mission: Impossible* TV series), **3.** waggly tail, **4.** piano, violin, flute, **5.** his father

Do You Know **WHAT**?

Take 20 points for each correct answer. Maximum this page: 100 points!

1. WHAT's a trunnel?
- a. A tunnel bored through especially soft stone
- b. A fresh-water fish of many colors
- c. proofreader's mark indicating removal of a stray character
- d. A wooden peg used in early house construction and in shipbuilding

2. WHAT's Jerolim?
- a. A Croatian island nudist beach
- b. A team of Israeli medical researchers
- c. A powerful Spanish liquor
- d. A Turkish mountain range

3. WHAT is the name of the giant rough diamond from which the Great Star of Africa and the Lesser Star of Africa—and a slew of smaller stones—were cut?
- a. Faraday
- b. Cullinan
- c. Johannesburg
- d. Super Star

4. WHAT is inscribed on the tip of Mont Blanc fountain pens?
- a. "3"—meaning Mont Blanc is a "triply good pen"
- b. "1911"—the year of Mont Blanc's founding
- c. "4810"—the approximate height (in meters) of the Mont
- d. The particular pen's recorded serial number

5. WHAT was the name of the bride in *My Big Fat Greek Wedding?*
- a. Angela
- b. Marina
- c. Christina
- d. Toula

SCORE FOR THIS TEST: _____ TOTAL SO FAR: _____

Do You Know **WHEN**?

Take 2 points for each correct answer. Maximum this page: 10 points!

1. WHEN does the Chattanooga Choo-Choo leave the Pennsylvania Station?
- a. At a little past nine
- b. 'Bout a quarter past eight
- c. 'Bout a quarter to four
- d. Whenever you like

2. "The Three Tenors"—José Carreras, Plácido Domingo, and Luciano Pavarotti—sang first at an outdoor performance in Rome, with Zubin Mehta conducting. WHEN?
- a. Summer of 1970
- b. Summer of 1980
- c. Summer of 1990
- d. Winter of 1991

3. WHEN did "YMCA," by the Village People, first hit it big?
- a. 1959
- b. 1978
- c. 1982
- d. 1990

4. WHEN did the Vienna Convention on Road Signs and Signals, standardizing signs, markings, and traffic lights, come into force?
- a. 1910
- b. 1946
- c. 1978
- d. 2000

5. "One Has My Name (The Other Has My Heart)" is—no surprise—a country song about tortured love. Jimmy Wakely first brought it to the top of the country charts. WHEN?
- a. 1948
- b. 1962
- c. 1969
- d. 1970

SCORE FOR THIS TEST: _____ TOTAL SO FAR: _____

ANSWERS: 1. c, 2. c, 3. b, 4. c, 5. a

Do You Know **HOW**?

Take 20 points for each correct answer. Maximum this page: 100 points!

1. HOW does an English billiards table differ from an American pool table?
- a. It has no pockets and the felt is blue, not green
- b. It's shorter
- c. It's longer, wider, and higher
- d. It doesn't

2. HOW did gypsy jazz guitar genius Django Reinhardt injure his fretting hand?
- a. A birth accident
- b. A mishap during his day job in a factory
- c. A fire in his caravan
- d. A botched armed robbery

3. Dutch elm disease is a fungal disease that has devastated elm trees in Europe and North America. HOW is it spread?
- a. By a specific beetle
- b. By several species of birds
- c. By squirrels
- d. By human contact

4. HOW do you recognize a deathwatch beetle?
- a. By its wine-like odor
- b. By its periodic tapping
- c. By its constant "snoring"
- d. By its cello-like bowing

5. HOW did seventeenth-century composer and conductor Jean-Baptiste Lully— Louis XIV's favorite music man—die?
- a. He was murdered by a jilted lover
- b. He was murdered by a rival composer
- c. He banged his baton on his big toe; it abscessed and he died from the infection
- d. He was bitten by the king's hunting dog, which had rabies

SCORE FOR THIS TEST: _____ TOTAL SO FAR: _____

ANSWERS: 1. c, 2. c, 3. a, 4. b, 5. c

Do You Know **AD SLOGANS**?

Take 10 points for each correct answer. Maximum this page: 50 points!

More memorable lines from advertising:

1. "Ring around the collar! Ring around the collar!"

a. Frosted Flakes

2. "How do you spell 'relief'?"

b. Shake 'n' Bake

3. "They're grrrreat!"

c. Dial

4. "And ah hayulped!"

d. Wisk

5. "Aren't you glad you use _____. Don't you wish everybody did?"

e. Rolaids

SCORE FOR THIS TEST: _____ TOTAL SO FAR: _____

Do You Know **IN COMMON**?

Take 20 points for each correct answer. Maximum this page: 100 points!

1. What do José Ferrer, Gérard Dépardieu, and Steve Martin have IN COMMON?

2. What do Benjamin Franklin, James Baldwin, and Sidney Bechet have IN COMMON?

3. What do André Agassi, John Amaechi, Tim Hardaway, and Tony Dungy have IN COMMON?

4. What do or did Alexander Scriabin, Lazar Berman, Vladimir Feltsman, and Evgeny Kissin have IN COMMON?

5. What do a novelty-song bandleader, the Partridges' mother, and Darth Vader's voice have IN COMMON?

SCORE FOR THIS TEST: _____ TOTAL SO FAR: _____

Do You Know **MATCHING QUIZ**?

Take 5 points for each correct answer. Maximum this page: 100 points!

1. MATCH the young ladies with the politicians who probably shouldn't have associated with them:

a. Fanne Fox

b. Donna Rice

c. Judith Exner

d. Elizabeth Ray

e. John F. Kennedy

f. Wayne Hays

g. Gary Hart

h. Wilbur Mills

2. MATCH the sobriquets with the Western heroes who carried them:

a. "King of the Cowboys"

b. "King of the Wild Frontier"

c. "O Henry's Robin Hood of the Old West"

d. "The Singing Cowboy"

e. Gene Autry

f. The Cisco Kid

g. Davy Crockett

h. Roy Rogers

3. MATCH the attackers with the injured:

a. Squeaky Fromme

b. Arthur Bremer Jr.

c. Mehmet Ali Agca

d. Valerie Solanas

e. Pope John Paul II

f. Andy Warhol

g. Gerald Ford

h. George Wallace

4. MATCH the TV characters with their occupations:

a. Quincy

b. Cliff Huxtable

c. Bob Hartley

d. Ben Casey

e. obstetrician

f. neurosurgeon

g. medical examiner

h. psychologist

5. MATCH some more TV characters with their jobs:

a. Jim Anderson

b. Elaine Nardo

c. George Jefferson

d. Steven Keaton

e. taxi driver

f. dry cleaner

g. public TV station manager

h. insurance salesman

SCORE FOR THIS TEST: _____ TOTAL SO FAR: _____

ANSWERS: 1. a-h, b-g, c-e, d-f, **2.** a-h, b-g, c-f, d-e, **3.** a-g, b-h, c-e, d-f, **4.** a-g *(Quincy, M.E.)*, b-e *(The Cosby Show)*, c-h *(The Bob Newhart Show)*, d-f *(Ben Casey)*, **5.** a-h *(Father Knows Best)*, b-e *(Taxi)*, c-f *(All in the Family, The Jeffersons)*, d-g *(Family Ties)*

Do You Know **TRUE OR FALSE**?

Take 4 points for each correct answer. Maximum this page: 20 points!

1. With all the hype about the dance, the song "Macarena," for which the dance was created, never made it above No. 52 on the U.S. pop charts.
_____ True   _____ False

2. Mr. Clean wears an earring.
_____ True   _____ False

3. Miss Moneypenny was James Bond's secretary.
_____ True   _____ False

4. Mr. Rogers was an ordained Presbyterian minister.
_____ True   _____ False

5. Before he got into the business of writing and drawing books for kids, Dr. Seuss was in the ad business. He created campaigns for an insecticide, including a slogan that was, for a few decades, much remembered and often parodied: "Quick, Henry, the Flit!"
_____ True   _____ False

SCORE FOR THIS TEST: _____ TOTAL SO FAR: _____

ANSWERS: 1. False (it was No. 1 for a more than respectable 14 weeks), **2.** True, **3.** False (she was secretary to Bond's boss, M, head of the British Secret Service), **4.** True, **5.** True

Do You Know **WHAT**?

Take 10 points for each correct answer. Maximum this page: 50 points!

1. In *2001: A Space Odyssey,* WHAT song does Hal, the supercomputer, sing just before he goes silent?

    a. "East Side, West Side"
    b. "Daisy Bell" ("A Bicycle Built for Two")
    c. "Always"
    d. "I Left My Heart in San Francisco"

2. WHAT does it mean, in hobo slang, to say someone "caught the westbound"?

    a. Died
    b. Gained a lot of weight
    c. Lost a lot of weight
    d. Moved to California

3. In our first view of Bogart in *Casablanca,* WHAT's he doing?

    a. Playing cards with Ugarte
    b. Playing cards with Sam
    c. Playing solitaire chess
    d. Noodling at Sam's piano

4. According to the ads, at 60 mph in a Rolls-Royce WHAT's the source of the loudest sound?

    a. The radio
    b. Your heartbeat
    c. The purr of your Siamese cat
    d. The dashboard clock

5. WHAT did "the man in the Hathaway shirt" wear above the neck?

    a. Sunglasses
    b. Monocle
    c. Eye patch
    d. Nose ring

SCORE FOR THIS TEST: _____ TOTAL SO FAR: _____

ANSWERS: 1. b, 2. a, 3. c, 4. d, 5. c

Do You Know **HOW MANY**?

Take 2 points for each correct answer. Maximum this page: 10 points!

1. In *Eight Is Enough,* Tom Bradford (Dick Van Patten) had eight sons and daughters. HOW MANY of each?

    a. One son, seven daughters
    b. Three sons, five daughters
    c. Five sons, three daughters
    d. Eight sons, no daughters

2. Before Wonder Bread advertised that it "builds strong bodies 12 ways," HOW MANY ways did it claim?

    a. 6
    b. 8
    c. 10
    d. 11

3. HOW MANY starring film roles did James Dean have?

    a. 2
    b. 3
    c. 5
    d. 6

4. "One Sweet Day," recorded by Mariah Carey and Boyz II Men, spent a record-breaking time at the top of the Billboard Hot 100 chart. HOW MANY weeks?

    a. 11
    b. 12
    c. 15
    d. 16

5. Simon, the early electronic game, had big buttons that lit up in sequence, each making a distinctive sound. HOW MANY buttons?

    a. 3
    b. 4
    c. 6
    d. 7

SCORE FOR THIS TEST: _____ TOTAL SO FAR: _____

ANSWERS: 1. b, **2.** b, **3.** b (*East of Eden, Rebel Without a Cause, Giant*) **4.** d, **5.** b (red, yellow, green, and blue)

Do You Know **WHEN**?

All or nothing: take 50 points for the whole shebang. Maximum this page: 50 points!

Who comes WHEN? Figure it out, and put these 10 names in chronological order, first to last.

1. Earl

2. Rudolph

3. Wilson

4. Baines

5. Milhous

6. David

7. Walker

8. Herbert Walker

9. Jefferson

10. Fitzgerald

SCORE FOR THIS TEST: _____ TOTAL SO FAR: _____

Do You Know **WHAT**?

Take 20 points for each correct answer. Maximum this page: 100 points!

1. WHAT song did Paul Anka write and record about his teen romance with Annette Funicello?

    a. "Diana"
    b. "You Are My Destiny"
    c. "I Miss You So"
    d. "Puppy Love"

2. The Orpheus Chamber Orchestra is best known for WHAT?

    a. Performing without a conductor
    b. Facing away from the audience
    c. Playing everything at half-tempo
    d. Singing while they play

3. Every collector of American coins wants an example of the 1909-SVDB Lincoln cent. The "S" is for the San Francisco mint. WHAT do the other letters stand for?

    a. A code for the date of first minting
    b. The designer's initials
    c. The mint director's initials
    d. Very Dark Bronze

4. WHAT was jazz giant Thelonious Monk's middle name?

    a. Adrian
    b. Potato
    c. Sphere
    d. Zoot

5. WHAT happened in ancient times at the Dome of the Rock in Jerusalem?

    a. Mohammed ascended to Allah
    b. Abraham offered to sacrifice his son Isaac
    c. Jesus negotiated with the Temple fathers
    d. The Hebrews regularly held wrestling matches

SCORE FOR THIS TEST: _____ TOTAL SO FAR: _____

Do You Know **FILL-IN QUIZ**?

Take 10 points for each correct answer. Maximum this page: 50 points!

1. "There is a fifth dimension beyond that which is known to man. . . . It is an area which we call _____ _____ _____."

2. "Look that up in your _____ _____ _____!"

3. "Up your nose with _____ _____ _____!"

4. Fats Domino found his thrill _____ _____ _____.

5. "Oh, no. It wasn't the airplanes. 'Twas Beauty _____ _____ _____."

SCORE FOR THIS TEST: _____ TOTAL SO FAR: _____

Do You Know **GRAB BAG**?

Take 10 points for each correct answer. Maximum this page: 50 points!

1. How did Peter Parker get his unusual abilities as Spider-Man?

2. In perhaps the most famous weekly episode of *Alfred Hitchcock Presents*, a woman bashes her husband's head in with a leg of lamb from the freezer. How does she dispose of the evidence?

3. E.T. learns English by watching what television show?

4. Why did Arthur Godfrey say he fired singer Julius La Rosa from his weekly program, *Arthur Godfrey and His Friends?*

5. Why did Virgil Starkweather fail as a bank robber?

SCORE FOR THIS TEST: _____ TOTAL SO FAR: _____

ANSWERS: 1. He was bitten by a radioactive spider, **2.** She serves it to the police investigators, **3.** *Sesame Street,* **4.** Godfrey said Julius had lost his humility, **5.** He sculpted a fake gun out of a bar of soap and, well, it rained (Woody Allen in *Take the Money and Run)*

Do You Know **WHO**?

Take 20 points for each correct answer. Maximum this page: 100 points!

1. On Columbus's first voyage of exploration, in 1492, WHO first sighted land?
   - a. The Santa Maria's medical officer
   - b. The cook aboard the Niña
   - c. A lookout aboard the Pinta
   - d. Columbus himself

2. WHO was Dr. Sivana?
   - a. A regular *Star Trek* villain
   - b. Captain Marvel's archenemy
   - c. Surgeon who performed the first heart transplant on a primate
   - d. Noted developer of hybrid peaches

3. WHO wrote the words used in the hymn "Amazing Grace"?
   - a. John Newton
   - b. Robert Frost
   - c. Billy Graham
   - d. Warren Peese

4. WHO was responsible for the fad for octagonal houses, built by the thousand in the nineteenth century?
   - a. George Bernard Shaw
   - b. Queen Victoria
   - c. Henry D. Thoreau
   - d. Orson S. Fowler

5. "The following program is brought to you in living color on NBC." WHO was the first to intone this, over a picture of a peacock?
   - a. John Cameron Swayze
   - b. Ben Grauer
   - c. Jack Benny
   - d. An unidentified announcer

SCORE FOR THIS TEST: _____ TOTAL SO FAR: _____

Do You Know **WHEN**?

Take 10 points for each correct answer. Maximum this page: 50 points!

What year did it happen?

1. First Sony Walkman released   **a.** 1954

2. Joe Namath chosen AFL rookie of the year   **b.** 1965

3. First of Tolkien's *Lord of the Rings* trilogy published   **c.** 1967

4. First small home microwave oven sold   **d.** 1979

5. *Challenger* space shuttle explodes   **e.** 1986

SCORE FOR THIS TEST: _____ TOTAL SO FAR: _____

ANSWERS: 1. d, 2. b, 3. a, 4. c, 5. e

Do You Know **WHERE**?

Take 4 points for each correct answer. Maximum this page: 20 points!

1. WHERE was this sweet little poem recited?

A little song, a little dance,
A little seltzer down your pants.

a. At the circus
b. At the White House
c. At Texas Stadium
d. At a funeral

2. WHERE did Bob Dylan grow up, mostly?

a. Brooklyn, New York
b. Nashville, Tennessee
c. Hibbing, Minnesota
d. Sydney, Australia

3. WHERE was Rick's Café Américain?

a. Paris
b. Bruges
c. Québec
d. Casablanca

4. WHERE can you stroll on a pedestrian-only street called Nanjing East Road?

a. Shanghai
b. Beijing
c. Vancouver
d. Seoul

5. And WHERE is the shopping avenue called Bahnhofstrasse?

a. Zürich
b. Hamburg
c. Vienna
d. Gstaad

SCORE FOR THIS TEST: _____ **TOTAL SO FAR:** _____

Answers: 1. d ("Chuckles the Clown" episode of *The Mary Tyler Moore Show*), 2. c, 3. d, 4. a, 5. a

Do You Know **COLORS**?

Take 10 points for each correct answer. Maximum this page: 50 points!

A color is in each of these:

1. "Godfather of Soul": _____ _____

2. Founder of Earth, Wind & Fire: _____ _____

3. Played Bobby Benson in the movie *The Day the Earth Stood Still* and Bud Anderson for years on *Father Knows Best:* _____ _____

4. Dodie Stevens song about her guy Dooley's clothes: "_____ _____ _____
_____ _____ _____ "

5. Perez Prado instrumental about apple blossoms, big in the fifties: "_____
_____ _____ _____ _____ _____ "

SCORE FOR THIS TEST: _____ TOTAL SO FAR: _____

ANSWERS: 1. James Brown, **2.** Maurice White, **3.** Billy Gray, **4.** "Tan Shoes and Pink Shoe Laces",
5. "Cherry Pink and Apple Blossom White"

Do You Know **COLORS**?

Take 10 points for each correct answer. Maximum this page: 50 points!

Some more questions on color:

1. Marty Robbins song about being all spiffed up: _____ _____ _____ (_____ _____ _____ _____)"

2. Movie notorious for line: "Don't you [bleepin'] look at me!": _____ _____

3. Hung from the church steeple in *The Longest Day:* _____ _____

4. Color of Pee Wee Herman's bowtie: _____

5. Smurf skin color: _____

SCORE FOR THIS TEST: _____ TOTAL SO FAR: _____

Do You Know **MUSIC HOBBYISTS**?

Take 20 points for each correct answer. Maximum this page: 100 points!

Match the notable personalities with the musical instruments they play:

1. Stephen King

a. saxophone

2. Woody Allen

b. guitar

3. Bill Clinton

c. banjo

4. Steve Martin

d. rhythm guitar

5. Adam Sandler

e. clarinet

SCORE FOR THIS TEST: _____ TOTAL SO FAR: _____

ANSWERS: 1. d, 2. e, 3. a, 4. c, 5. b

Do You Know **MUSIC HOBBYISTS**?

Take 20 points for each correct answer. Maximum this page: 100 points!

More celebrities and their instruments:

1. Drew Carey   **a.** accordion

2. Prince Charles   **b.** drums

3. Emeril Lagasse   **c.** trumpet

4. Meryl Streep   **d.** cello

5. Deborah Norville   **e.** violin

SCORE FOR THIS TEST: _____ TOTAL SO FAR: _____

ANSWERS: 1. c, **2.** d, **3.** b, **4.** e, **5.** a

Do You Know **WHICH**?

Take 10 points for each correct answer. Maximum this page: 50 points!

1. WHICH tennis player won the U.S. Open on all three surfaces: grass, Har-Tru clay, and DecoTurf?
- a. John McEnroe
- b. Jimmy Connors
- c. Arthur Ashe
- d. Vic Seixas

2. WHICH animal boasts the longest maximum lifespan in captivity?
- a. Chicken
- b. Chimpanzee
- c. Goldfish
- d. Housefly

3. WHICH U.S. President had a retreat named Poplar Forest?
- a. Thomas Jefferson
- b. Andrew Johnson
- c. Theodore Roosevelt
- d. Harry Truman

4. WHICH Hemingway title derives from the Biblical book of "Ecclesiastes"?
- a. *To Have and Have Not*
- b. *For Whom the Bell Tolls*
- c. *A Moveable Feast*
- d. *The Sun Also Rises*

5. In WHICH game would you regularly encounter a *telltale?*
- a. Badminton
- b. Squash
- c. Chess
- d. Snooker

SCORE FOR THIS TEST: _____ TOTAL SO FAR: _____

Do You Know **WHICH—ODD ONE OUT**?

Take 10 points for each correct answer. Maximum this page: 50 points!

1. WHICH country has a national flag that *isn't* red, white, and blue?

    a. France
    b. Italy
    c. Netherlands
    d. North Korea

2. WHICH racehorse *wasn't* destroyed after a running accident?

    a. Secretariat
    b. Ruffian
    c. Barbaro
    d. Horatio Nelson

3. WHICH work did Picasso *not* paint?

    a. *Guernica*
    b. *The Weeping Woman*
    c. *The Old Guitarist*
    d. *View of Toledo*

4. WHICH of these bones or muscles *isn't* in the chest?

    a. Clavicle
    b. Tibia
    c. Sternum
    d. Pectoral

5. Originally, the Chicago Seven were the Chicago Eight, but one of the 1968 antiwar defendants was tried separately. WHICH?

    a. Rennie Davis
    b. David Dellinger
    c. John Froines
    d. Tom Hayden
    e. Abbie Hoffman
    f. Jerry Rubin
    g. Bobby Seale
    h. Lee Weiner

SCORE FOR THIS TEST: _____ TOTAL SO FAR: _____

Do You Know **WHAT**?

Take 20 points for each correct answer. Maximum this page: 100 points!

1. WHAT was the occupation of Jack Ruby, the man who shot JFK assassin Lee Harvey Oswald?

    a. Bartender
    b. High school principal
    c. Nightclub owner
    d. Schoolbook publisher

2. WHAT was Humphrey Bogart character Charley All-nut's occupation? (The role brought Bogie his only Oscar.)

    a. Prospector
    b. Boat captain
    c. Private investigator
    d. Chef

3. Rachel Carson's book *Silent Spring* sounded an early environmental alarm. WHAT was Carson's training?

    a. Arborist
    b. Botanist
    c. Dentist
    d. Marine biologist

4. Sidney Franklin was the first American to become prominent in Latin America and Spain as a successful WHAT?

    a. Bullfighter
    b. Pop singer
    c. Mercenary
    d. Ophthalmologist

5. WHAT was the day job of Dashiell Hammett, creator of *Sam Spade* and *The Thin Man?*

    a. Radio announcer
    b. Comic book artist
    c. Detective
    d. Tax auditor

SCORE FOR THIS TEST: _____ TOTAL SO FAR: _____

Do You Know **FILL-IN QUIZ**?

Take 10 points for each correct answer. Maximum this page: 50 points!

1. Omar Sharif's card game: _____.

2. The youngest Beatle: _____ _____.

3. Child preacher who spilled the beans about the profitable business of evangelical revival shows in a documentary film named for him: _____ _____.

4. "Good night, Chet." "Good night, _____."

5. She starred with Elvis in *Loving You* and *King Creole,* and in the spring break classic, *Where the Boys Are.* Then she left the business and became a nun. She's _____ _____.

SCORE FOR THIS TEST: _____ TOTAL SO FAR: _____

ANSWERS: 1. Bridge (once a top player, he wrote books and a newspaper column on the game), **2. George Harrison, 3. Marjoe Gortner** (the film was *Marjoe*), **4. David** (Chet Huntley and David Brinkley on *The Huntley-Brinkley Report*), **5. Dolores Hart**

Do You Know **WHEN**?

Take 20 points for each correct answer. Maximum this page: 100 points!

1. WHEN was John Lennon shot?
- a. 1976
- b. 1978
- c. 1980
- d. 1985

2. WHEN did wire nails—the round-shank nails commonly used today—take over in the building trade?
- a. About 1600
- b. About 1800
- c. About 1900
- d. About 1950

3. WHEN was *Star Wars* released?
- a. 1968
- b. 1977
- c. 1988
- d. 1989

4. WHEN, according to Al Jolson, will the stars twinkle and shine?
- a. 6:00
- b. 7:00
- c. 8:45
- d. Midnight

5. "WHEN it's eight, nine, ten, eleven too," what will Bill Haley be doing?
- a. "I'll be goin' strong, and so will you."
- b. "I'll be comin' for ya, and I'll love ya true."
- c. "I'll be lovin' you, baby, and your cousin Sue."
- d. "I'll be tappin' a keg and pumpin' the brew."

SCORE FOR THIS TEST: _____ TOTAL SO FAR: _____

Do You Know **POP SONGS' CLASSICAL ORIGINS**?

Take 20 points for each correct answer. Maximum this page: 100 points!

Match the classical composers with the popular songs taken from their works:

1. "I'm Always Chasing Rainbows"   a. Dvořák

2. "Hello Muddah, Hello Faddah"   b. Wagner

3. "Goin' Home"   c. Ponchielli

4. "Here Comes the Bride"   d. Chopin

5. "Till the End of Time"   e. Chopin

SCORE FOR THIS TEST: _____   TOTAL SO FAR: _____

Do You Know **MOVIE ENDINGS**?

Take 10 points for each correct answer. Maximum this page: 50 points!

Some more lines and the films they ended:

1. " . . . There's no place like home."

   a. *Some Like It Hot*

2. "All right, Mr. DeMille, I'm ready for my close-up."

   b. *On Golden Pond*

3. "Wanna dance, or would you rather just suck face?"

   c. *Casablanca*

4. "Well, nobody's perfect."

   d. *Sunset Boulevard*

5. "Louis, I think is the beginning of a beautiful friendship."

   e. *The Wizard of Oz*

SCORE FOR THIS TEST: _____ TOTAL SO FAR: _____

Do You Know **MOVIE ENDINGS**?

Take 10 points for each correct answer. Maximum this page: 50 points!

And yet more last lines:

1. "In spite of everything, I still believe that people are really good at heart."

   a. *Dr. Strangelove*

2. " . . . They'll say, 'Why she wouldn't even hurt a fly!'"

   b. *The Diary of Anne Frank*

3. "Mein Führer—I can walk!"

   c. *Cabaret*

4. "Sing it out, men! Higher, you animals, higher! We open in Leavenworth Saturday night!"

   d. *The Producers*

5. "Here, life is beautiful. The girls are beautiful. Even the orchestra is beautiful. *Auf Wiedersehen! A bientôt.*"

   e. *Psycho*

SCORE FOR THIS TEST: _____ TOTAL SO FAR: _____

ANSWERS: 1. b, 2. e, 3. a, 4. d, 5. c

Do You Know **WHAT**?

Take 10 points for each correct answer. Maximum this page: 50 points!

1. WHAT product was sold in commercials with this line: "I'm not a doctor, but I play one on TV . . ."?

- a. Anacin
- b. Tylenol
- c. Vicks Formula 44
- d. Pall Mall

2. WHAT fad toy did ad man Gary Dahl dream up in 1975?

- a. The Pet Rock
- b. Tickle Me Elmo
- c. Pop Rocks
- d. The Slinky

3. WHAT was Patricia Hearst's nickname after she was kidnapped and briefly became a revolutionary?

- a. Field Marshal Cinque
- b. Tanya
- c. Patty-hoo
- d. Squeaky

4. If you have a wood-handled tool, like a hammer or hatchet, odds are the wood is WHAT?

- a. Beech
- b. Hickory
- c. Southern Magnolia
- d. White Oak

5. Before his solo career, Lionel Richie was a member of WHAT group?

- a. The Angels
- b. Genesis
- c. Blood, Sweat, and Tears
- d. The Commodores

SCORE FOR THIS TEST: _____ TOTAL SO FAR: _____

Do You Know **WHERE**?

Take 20 points for each correct answer. Maximum this page: 100 points!

1. WHERE might you hear people mention the terms *penultimate* and *rover?*

    a. At an auto dealership
    b. On a cricket pitch
    c. In a concert hall
    d. In a gold mine

2. WHERE were artificial harbors called mulberries used in warfare?

    a. At Omaha Beach, during World War II
    b. At Troy, during the Trojan Wars
    c. At Dien Bien Phu, in the first Indochina War
    d. In Grenada, during the U.S. invasion of 1983

3. WHERE are you most likely to find *mititei* on a menu?

    a. Italy
    b. Romania
    c. West Indies
    d. New Zealand

4. WHERE might you see people practicing spirals, spread-eagles, snowplows, and T-stops?

    a. A dental school
    b. A horse rink
    c. A wrestling ring
    d. An ice skating rink

5. And WHERE might you see a demi-plié and a cramp roll?

    a. A bakery
    b. An auto repair shop
    c. A dance studio
    d. A planetarium

SCORE FOR THIS TEST: _____ TOTAL SO FAR: _____

Do You Know **FILL-IN QUIZ**?

Take 10 points for each correct answer. Maximum this page: 50 points!

1. "Maxwell Edison, majoring in _____."

2. "Baby, you're _____ _____!"

3. F. Murray Abraham envied Tom Hulce's beautiful creations in _____.

4. Janitor who discovered Watergate break-in and called cops: _____ _____.

5. "Who Shot _____ _____?"

SCORE FOR THIS TEST: _____ **TOTAL SO FAR:** _____

ANSWERS: 1. medicine (Beatles song "Maxwell's Silver Hammer"), **2.** the greatest (Ralph Kramden to Alice in *The Honeymooners*), **3.** *Amadeus*, **4.** Frank Wills, **5.** J.R. (*Dallas*)

Do You Know **WHAT**?

Take 10 points for each correct answer. Maximum this page: 50 points!

1. WHAT do the letters "BMW" on the car stand for?
- a. Bavarian Master World
- b. Brilliant Motor Workshop
- c. Bradley Made Weapon
- d. Bayerische Motoren Werke

2. On an official major league baseball diamond, WHAT's the distance from the pitcher's mound to home plate?
- a. 60 feet, 6 inches
- b. 58 feet
- c. 20 meters
- d. 44 feet

3. WHAT's the name of the facility where Cabbage Patch Kids are "born"?
- a. Babyland General Hospital
- b. Cole Garden Medical Center
- c. The Small Doll Clinic
- d. Georgia State Health Home for Miniatures

4. WHAT song was used in Heinz ketchup commercials in the seventies?
- a. "Good Vibrations" (The Beach Boys)
- b. "The 59th Street Bridge Song (Feelin' Groovy)" (Simon & Garfunkel)
- c. "Anticipation" (Carly Simon)
- d. "Let It Be" (The Beatles)

5. Before Wham-O started making the Frisbee in the 1950s, WHAT was the flying disc called?
- a. Pie Plate
- b. Pluto Platter
- c. Saucy Saucer
- d. Zapper

SCORE FOR THIS TEST: _____ TOTAL SO FAR: _____

Do You Know **WHEN**?

Take 10 points for each correct answer. Maximum this page: 50 points!

What year did it happen?

1. Pac-Man hits America   **a.** 1957

2. *American Bandstand* goes national   **b.** 1969

3. Rolling Stones play Altamont   **c.** 1974

4. Cosby starts pitching Jell-O   **d.** 1980

5. *M*A*S*H* airs final episode   **e.** 1983

SCORE FOR THIS TEST: _____ TOTAL SO FAR: _____

Do You Know **SEINFELD**?

Take 10 points for each correct answer. Maximum this page: 50 points!

Match the secondary *Seinfeld* characters with the way they paid the rent:

1. Kenny Bania   **a.** comedian

2. Tim Whatleigh   **b.** lawyer

3. Jackie Chiles   **c.** restaurateur

4. Poppy   **d.** postman

5. Newman   **e.** dentist

SCORE FOR THIS TEST: _____ TOTAL SO FAR: _____

Do You Know **FASHION BRANDS**?

Take 10 points for each correct answer. Maximum this page: 50 points!

Match the brands and the products found in fine clothing stores:

1. Thomas Pink

a. men's hats

2. Manola Blahnik

b. men's suits

3. Bottega Veneta

c. men's shirts

4. Giorgio Amani

d. women's handbags

5. Borsalino

e. women's shoes

SCORE FOR THIS TEST: _____ TOTAL SO FAR: _____

Do You Know IN COMMON?

Take 20 points for each correct answer. Maximum this page: 100 points!

1. What do (or did) Howard Cosell, Geraldo Rivera, Charlie Rose, Mahatma Gandhi, and Fidel Castro have IN COMMON?

2. What did Pete Best and Stu Sutcliff have IN COMMON?

3. What do Mike Tyson, Sophia Loren, Kelsey Grammer, and Dwight Gooden have IN COMMON?

4. What do Barbra Streisand, Dustin Hoffman, and Robin Williams have IN COMMON?

5. What did Wild Bill Hickok and Al Jolson have IN COMMON?

SCORE FOR THIS TEST: _____ TOTAL SO FAR: _____

ANSWERS: 1. A law degree, **2.** One-time membership in the Beatles, **3.** Time in jail, **4.** Cross-dressed on the big screen (Streisand in *Yentl*, Hoffman in *Tootsie*, Williams in *Mrs. Doubtfire*), **5.** Died playing cards (Hickok held the poker player's "dead man's hand," a pair of aces and a pair of eights; Jolson, playing gin rummy with pals, said "Boys, I'm going . . .")

Do You Know **FILL-IN QUIZ**?

Take 10 points for each correct answer. Maximum this page: 50 points!

1. Boris Karloff in *Bride of Frankenstein:* "We belong _____."

2. A pony named Macaroni and a Springer spaniel named Millie both lived in

_____ _____ _____.

3. French fries covered with cheese curds and hot gravy, in Montréal: _____.

4. A radio funnyman who faux-feuded with Jack Benny, a multi-talented early TV talker, and "The Tool Man" on *Home Improvement* had the same last name:

_____.

5. "We don't need no stinkin' badges!" The original movie line, a little more elaborate, was: "Badges? We ain't got no badges. We don't need no badges! I don't have to show you any stinkin' badges!" It's from the Humphrey Bogart flick _____ _____ _____ _____ _____.

SCORE FOR THIS TEST: _____ TOTAL SO FAR: _____

Do You Know **WHO**?

Take 10 points for each correct answer. Maximum this page: 50 points!

1. In 1960, not yet 15, Kathy Young recorded "A Thousand Stars." WHO sang backup?

    a. The Asteroids
    b. The Futuramas
    c. The Clifftones
    d. The Innocents

2. WHO wrote the lyrics for Gilbert and Sullivan operettas?

    a. Gilbert
    b. Sullivan
    c. Both
    d. A third, unnamed collaborator

3. In 1949, Louis Armstrong became the first jazz musician to make the cover of *Time* magazine. WHO, in 1954, was second?

    a. Duke Ellington
    b. Dave Brubeck
    c. Miles Davis
    d. Charlie Parker

4. Al Jolson's spot in movie history was clinched by his role in *The Jazz Singer,* often called the "first talkie." Jolson landed the part after the song-and-dance man who had launched the role on stage demanded too much money for the film version. WHO was that?

    a. Rudy Vallee
    b. Jack Pepper
    c. Walter Winchell
    d. George Jessel

5. WHO sang the theme song from *High Noon?* ("Do not forsake me, oh my darlin.' . . .")

    a. Gary Cooper
    b. Frankie Laine
    c. Tex Ritter
    d. Lloyd Bridges

SCORE FOR THIS TEST: _____ TOTAL SO FAR: _____

ANSWERS: 1. d, 2. a, 3. b, 4. d, 5. c

Do You Know **WHAT'S GOING ON**?

Take 10 points for each correct answer. Maximum this page: 50 points!

1. "Something beyond comprehension is happening to a little girl on this street, in this house. . . . A man has been called for as a last resort, to try and save her." WHAT'S GOING ON?

2. October 30, 1938. *Mercury Theatre* is on the radio, and people are anxiously phoning their local stations. WHAT'S GOING ON?

3. May 1, 1960. A U-2 is down. WHAT'S GOING ON?

4. The August 1962 issue of *Amazing Fantasy* (No. 15) is on the stands. WHAT'S GOING ON?

5. Whenever you and I argue it really tears me apart. Why? Because I panic, thinking we might split up. So every evening I look up at the sky and ask, "Hey, how come I gotta be a lovesick adolescent?" WHAT'S GOING ON?

SCORE FOR THIS TEST: _____ TOTAL SO FAR: _____

ANSWERS: 1. *The Exorcist*, **2.** The Orson Welles version of "The War of the Worlds" with Martians invading New Jersey, **3.** U.S. spy plane, and its pilot, Gary Powers, shot down over Soviet territory, **4.** Debut of Spider-Man, **5.** As Dion (singing with the Belmonts) put it: "Each time we have a quarrel, It almost breaks my heart, 'Cause I am so afraid, That we will have to part. Each night I ask the stars up above: 'Why must I be a Teenager in Love?'"

Do You Know **IN COMMON**?

Take 20 points for each correct answer. Maximum this page: 100 points!

1. What do Ray Barone and Oscar Madison have IN COMMON?

2. What do Mike Brady and Elyse Keaton have IN COMMON?

3. What do Jack Nicholson, Robert De Niro, and Jon Lovitz have IN COMMON? (Hint: Someone made them do it.)

4. What do Bill Clinton, George H.W. Bush, Ronald Reagan, Gerald Ford, Paul McCartney, and Ringo Starr have IN COMMON? (Hint: It's not right.)

5. What do Harpo Marx, Yul Brynner, and Mickey Mouse have IN COMMON? (Hint: "An' a-one, an' a-two . . .")

SCORE FOR THIS TEST: _____ **TOTAL SO FAR:** _____

Do You Know **WHAT**?

Take 2 points for each correct answer. Maximum this page: 10 points!

1. On *Wonder Years,* WHAT did Wayne call Kevin?

    a. Li'l Bro
    b. Butthead
    c. Beavis
    d. Kevvy-Baby

2. WHAT's the name of the character played by Michael Douglas in his Oscar-winning role in *Wall Street?*

    a. Gary Gekker
    b. Gordon Gekko
    c. Harry Milken
    d. Gore DePalma

3. WHAT dance was described in song as "a graveyard smash" that "caught on in a flash"?

    a. "Sinister Stomp"
    b. "Your Hoodoo Man"
    c. "Transylvania Twist"
    d. "Monster Mash"

4. WHAT is an Uzi?

    a. An Italian pastry
    b. A museum in Rio de Janeiro
    c. An Israeli submachine gun
    d. On *Star Trek,* an inhabitant of the Planet Dweeb

5. WHAT airline used The Fifth Dimension's "Up, Up, and Away" in its commercials?

    a. TWA
    b. Pan Am
    c. British Airways
    d. American Airlines

SCORE FOR THIS TEST: _____ TOTAL SO FAR: _____

ANSWERS: 1. b, 2. b, 3. d, 4. c, 5. a

Do You Know **REAL NAMES**?

Take 10 points for each correct answer. Maximum this page: 50 points!

Pair the celebrities on the left with their pre-showbiz names on the right:

1. Boris Karloff

a. Carlos Estévez

2. Robert Blake

b. Caryn Johnson

3. Jamie Foxx

c. Michael Gubitosi

4. Whoopi Goldberg

d. William Henry Pratt

5. Charlie Sheen

e. Eric Morlon Bishop

SCORE FOR THIS TEST: _____ TOTAL SO FAR: _____

Do You Know **REAL NAMES**?

Take 10 points for each correct answer. Maximum this page: 50 points!

More celebrities and their real names:

1. Jon Stewart

a. Lawrence Zeiger

2. Alice Cooper

b. William Bailey

3. Buckwheat Zydeco

c. Vincent Fournier

4. Larry King

d. Jonathan Leibowitz

5. Axl Rose

e. Stanley Dural Jr.

SCORE FOR THIS TEST: _____ TOTAL SO FAR: _____

Do You Know **FOOD AND DRINK**?

Take 10 points for each correct answer. Maximum this page: 50 points!

1. What French sweet, taken with tea, set Marcel Proust to reminiscing?
- a. Éclair
- b. Pain au chocolat
- c. Mille-feuille
- d. Madeleine

3. What's the fruit ingredient in the cocktail called a Bellini?
- a. Apple
- b. Pear
- c. Peach
- d. Kiwi

4. Which isn't normally an ingredient in egg rolls?
- a. Pork
- b, Bean sprouts
- c. Celery
- d. Egg

2. What shape is Camembert cheese?
- a. Round
- b. Square
- c. Trapezoidal
- d. Cylindrical

5. And which juice isn't in V-8 Juice?
- a. Tomato
- b. Carrot
- c. Pepper
- d. Celery
- e. Beet
- f. Parsley
- g. Lettuce
- h. Watercress
- i. Spinach

SCORE FOR THIS TEST: _____ TOTAL SO FAR: _____

Do You Know **FILL-IN QUIZ**?

Take 20 points for each correct answer. Maximum this page: 100 points!

1. Toonces the _____ _____.

2. Vodka, triple sec, and cranberry juice make a _____.

3. "When you pay off the first baseman every month, who gets the money?" "Every dollar of it." That's part of a classic comedy routine called "_____ _____ _____?"

4. The Queen of Rock 'n' Roll, an actress discovered at Schwab's Drug Store, and the founder of CNN. Same last name: _____.

5. Casey Stengel's real first and middle names: _____ _____.

SCORE FOR THIS TEST: _____ TOTAL SO FAR: _____

ANSWERS: 1. Driving Cat (*Saturday Night Live*), **2.** Cosmopolitan, **3** "Who's on First?" (Abbott and Costello), **4.** Turner (Tina, Lana, and Ted), **5.** Charles Dillon (the New York Yankees manager)

Do You Know **WHAT**?

Take 10 points for each correct answer. Maximum this page: 50 points!

1. According to the Bible, WHAT musical instrument did King David play?
- a. Harp
- b. Lyre
- c. Nose flute
- d. Clarinet

2. Composer-arranger Marvin Hamlisch turned the music of Scott Joplin into an Oscar-winning score. For WHAT movie?
- a. "The Entertainer"
- b. "The Sting"
- c. "The Way We Were"
- d. "Ragtime"

3. WHAT twist on the catchphrase "Elvis has left the building" was used at the end of episodes of a TV series?
- a. "Liberace has left the building"
- b. "Mr. T has left the building"
- c. "Frasier has left the building"
- d. "Maude has left the building"

4. WHAT are the most notable facial characteristics of the wizard Gandalf?
- a. An enormous nose
- b. Tri-tone skin
- c. A third eye in his forehead, usually hidden by his hat
- d. Bushy eyebrows and a long beard

5. WHAT was the name of Madonna's first album?
- a. "Madonna"
- b. "Like a Virgin"
- c. "You Can Dance"
- d. "Erotica"

SCORE FOR THIS TEST: _____ TOTAL SO FAR: _____

Do You Know **THE BOSS'S PLACE**?

Take 10 points for each correct answer. Maximum this page: 50 points!

Match the countries to the leaders' official residences:

1. Elysée

a. Spain

2. Bellevue

b. Australia

3. Chigi

c. France

4. Moncloa

d. Italy

5. Lodge

e. Germany

SCORE FOR THIS TEST: _____ TOTAL SO FAR: _____

Do You Know **WHAT THEIR PUBLICISTS CALLED THEM**?

Take 10 points for each correct answer. Maximum this page: 50 points!

Match the actresses to their publicity department monikers:

1. "The Sweater Girl"

a. Ann Sheridan

2. "The 'It' Girl"

b. Jean Harlow

3. "The 'Oomph' Girl"

c. Clara Bow

4. "The Platinum Blonde"

d. Marie McDonald

5. "The Body"

e. Lana Turner

SCORE FOR THIS TEST: _____ TOTAL SO FAR: _____

Do You Know **WHO**?

Take 4 points for each correct answer. Maximum this page: 20 points!

1. WHO, in comics, has a girlfriend named Daisy and a cousin Gladstone?
- a. Donald Duck
- b. Elmer Fudd
- c. Green Arrow
- d. Pluto

2. Michael Jackson was rumored to have offered $50,000 for a man's bones. WHO?
- a. Hitler
- b. Napoleon
- c. The Elephant Man
- d. Elvis

3. WHO got "cards and letters from people I don't even know"?
- a. Liberace, after his first TV appearance
- b. Glenn Campbell, singing "Rhinestone Cowboy"
- c. Ivan Lendl, after his first U.S. Open win
- d. Ronald Reagan, while he was governor of California

5. WHO collects royalties on Irving Berlin's "God Bless America"?
- a. The Boy Scouts and Girl Scouts
- b. Michael Jackson
- c. Berlin's estate
- d. No one—the song is in the public domain, so it's royalty-free

4. WHO was Jackie Paper's best friend?
- a. Tarzan of the Apes
- b. Puff the Magic Dragon
- c. Fritzie Ritz
- d. Honey Honalee

SCORE FOR THIS TEST: _____ TOTAL SO FAR: _____

Do You Know **WHERE**?

Take 10 points for each correct answer. Maximum this page: 50 points!

1. WHERE did Ben and Jerry open their first ice cream parlor?
- a. A former Army-Navy store in Queens, New York
- b. A former strip joint in Cambridge, Massachusetts
- c. A former Burger King in Putney, Vermont
- d. A former gas station in Burlington, Vermont

2. WHERE does the story of the Dybbuk, the wandering soul of a dead person, come from?
- a. A Chinese folk tale
- b. An oral tradition of West Africa
- c. A Jewish legend from medieval Eastern Europe
- d. A 20th-century playwright's imagination

3. WHERE did Conan the Barbarian call home?
- a. Cimmeria
- b. Atlantis
- c. Ireland
- d. Conania

4. WHERE would you expect to find a mandoline?
- a. A library
- b. A kitchen
- c. A clothes closet
- d. An orchestral practice room

5. WHERE can you stand on a bridge known as the Bridge of Sighs?
- a. Venice
- b. Oxford
- c. Cambridge
- d. Frankfurt
- e. all of the above

SCORE FOR THIS TEST: _____ TOTAL SO FAR: _____

Do You Know **WHICH**?

Take 20 points for each correct answer. Maximum this page: 100 points!

1. WHICH city is northernmost?
- a. Barcelona
- b. Naples
- c. Sacramento
- d. Tokyo

2. WHICH has Dr. Dre been associated with?
- a. The rap group N.W.A.
- b. Eminem
- c. Snoop Doggy Dogg
- d. Death Row Records
- e. all of the above

3. WHICH English author wrote the novel that was loosely adapted into the movie *Clueless?*
- a. Anne Brontë
- b. Charlotte Brontë
- c. Emily Brontë
- d. Jane Austen

4. Bob Dylan made his recording debut playing harmonica with WHICH singer?
- a. Harry Belafonte
- b. Willie Nelson
- c. Eddie Fisher
- d. Little Richard

5. WHICH Metropolis newspaper did Clark Kent work for before he landed a job at *The Daily Planet?*
- a. *The Metropolis Gazette*
- b. *The Daily Star*
- c. *The Evening Post*
- d. *The Morning Chief*

SCORE FOR THIS TEST: _____ TOTAL SO FAR: _____

Do You Know **WHICH—ODD ONE OUT**?

Take 4 points for each correct answer. Maximum this page: 20 points!

1. In *Dr. Strangelove*, WHICH role *didn't* Peter Sellers play?
   a. Dr. Strangelove
   b. President Merkin Muffley
   c. Major T.J. "King" Kong
   d. Group Captain Lionel Mandrake

2. WHICH animals are the Galápagos Islands *not* noted for?
   a. Manatee
   b. Marine iguana
   c. Giant tortoise
   d. Blue-footed booby

3. WHICH railroad *doesn't* rate a space on the Monopoly board?
   a. Pennsylvania
   b. B&O
   c. Short Line
   d. Reading
   e. Dover Special

4. In *Casablanca*, WHICH song *didn't* Sam sing?
   a. "As Time Goes By"
   b. "It Had to Be You"
   c. "Shine"
   d. "La Vie en Rose"
   e. "Knock on Wood"

5. Larry Fine and Moe Howard were the long-lasting members of The Three Stooges. WHICH of these *never* filled the third slot?
   a. Shemp
   b. Curly
   c. Baldy
   d. Joe
   e. Curly Joe

SCORE FOR THIS TEST: _____ TOTAL SO FAR: _____

Do You Know **WHAT**?

1. WHAT was baseball pitching great Satchel Paige's real first name?

    a. Leroy
    b. Walter
    c. Sander
    d. Satchel

2. The ball used in court handball is made of WHAT?

    a. Rubber
    b. Celluloid
    c. Any of five species of tree
    d. Cork and nylon

3. When Boston Celtics coach Arnold "Red" Auerbach thought his team had clinched another victory, he did WHAT?

    a. Stood up and hollered, "WE DID IT, GUYS!"
    b. Sat on the floor and spun in circles
    c. Lit a cigar
    d. Tugged his right ear

4. WHAT's been called "the most exciting two minutes in sports"?

    a. The end of any NBA overtime
    b. The Kentucky Derby
    c. Olympic men's 1,000-meter
    d. Start of a roller derby jam

5. WHAT does "NASCAR" stand for?

    a. North American Society of Cooperative Auto Racers
    b. National Auto Society, Cars And Races
    c. National Association for Stock Car Auto Racing
    d. National Affiliated Stock Car Association, Regulated

SCORE FOR THIS TEST: _____ TOTAL SO FAR: _____

Do You Know **FILL-IN QUIZ**?

Take 10 points for each correct answer. Maximum this page: 50 points!

1. In the online text world, AAMOF means _____ _____ _____ _____ _____.

2. Before his singing career took off, Perry Como was a _____.

3. Played on TV by Jack Larson, Jimmy Olsen, cub reporter at *The Daily Planet*, always wore a _____.

4. Chief product of the city of Villedieu-les-Poêles, France: _____.

5. Gang always after $crooge McDuck's zillions: The _____ _____.

SCORE FOR THIS TEST: _____ **TOTAL SO FAR:** _____

Do You Know **WORLD HOTELS**?

Take 20 points for each correct answer. Maximum this page: 100 points!

Match the cities to the luxury hotels with the English-sounding names:

1. Carlyle

a. Rome

2. Bristol

b. New York

3. Regent

c. Athens

4. Eden

d. Hong Kong

5. King George

e. Paris

SCORE FOR THIS TEST: _____ TOTAL SO FAR: _____

Do You Know **TV LINES**?

Take 10 points for each correct answer. Maximum this page: 50 points!

Match the regular lines to the folks who said them:

1. "Well, isn't that special?"

a. Rod Roddy

2. "Come on down!"

b. Bart Simpson

3. "Afternoon, everybody!"

c. Sophia Petrillo

4. "Picture it: Sicily, 1932 . . ."

d. Norm Peterson

5. "Eat my shorts!"

e. The Church Lady

SCORE FOR THIS TEST: _____ TOTAL SO FAR: _____

Do You Know **WHAT**?

Take 4 points for each correct answer. Maximum this page: 20 points!

1. Hollywood's top dog first appeared in a children's book. WHAT's its title?
- a. *Here, Lassie!*
- b. *Courage of Lassie*
- c. *The Adventures of Lassie*
- d. *Lassie Come Home*

2. According to the folk song popularized by the Kingston Trio, from WHAT kind of tree would Tom Dooley hang?
- a. A tall pine
- b. A white oak
- c. A green apple
- d. A huckleberry

3. In *How to Steal a Million,* starring Audrey Hepburn, Peter O'Toole, and Charles Boyer, WHAT was the object of the grand theft?
- a. A racehorse
- b. Jewelry
- c. Art
- d. Cash

4. WHAT's the chief symbol of Wicca, the neo-pagan, nature-based religion?
- a. A circle in a five-pointed star
- b. A circle in a six-pointed star
- c. A five-pointed star in a circle
- d. A six-pointed star in a circle

5. If Elvis didn't want to be a tiger or a lion (the former "play too rough"; the latter "ain't the kind you love enough"), WHAT did he want to be?
- a. Your teddy bear
- b. Your pussycat
- c. Your cuddly pup
- d. Your kangaroo-roo-roo

SCORE FOR THIS TEST: _____ TOTAL SO FAR: _____

Do You Know **HOW**?

Take 10 points for each correct answer. Maximum this page: 50 points!

1. HOW old was Jerry Lee Lewis's cousin when they were married?

    a. 12
    b. 13
    c. 14
    d. 15

2. HOW much did a ticket to Woodstock cost?

    a. $18
    b. $25
    c. $36
    d. $100

3. HOW long is the Camptown Racetrack?

    a. 1 mile and a furlong
    b. 2 miles and two furlongs
    c. 5 miles
    d. 9 miles

4. HOW tall was the shortest NBA player ever to win MVP?

    a. 5'7"
    b. 5'9"
    c. 6'0"
    d. 6'2"

5. HOW old was Einstein when he developed the special theory of relativity?

    a. 18
    b. 26
    c. 50
    d. 81

SCORE FOR THIS TEST: _____ **TOTAL SO FAR:** _____

Do You Know **WHO**?

Take 20 points for each correct answer. Maximum this page: 100 points!

1. WHO said "War, war, war. This war talk's spoiling all the fun at every party this spring. I get so bored I could scream."
- a. Paris Hilton
- b. Tony Danza
- c. Richard Simmons
- d. Scarlett O'Hara

2. WHO were the two heavyweight boxing champs immediately preceding Cassius Clay, who won the crown in 1964?
- a. Sonny Liston and Ingemar Johansson
- b. Floyd Patterson and Sonny Liston
- c. Floyd Patterson and Ingemar Johansson
- d. Sonny Liston and Rocky Marciano

4. WHO wrote "Mary Had a Little Lamb"?
- a. Emily Dickinson
- b. Ogden Nash
- c. Sarah Josepha Hale
- d. The author is unknown

3. WHO was an audience regular at the Jack Paar and Merv Griffin programs, often acknowledged by the host?
- a. Mrs. Miller
- b. Mrs. Sylvester
- c. Mrs. De Cordova
- d. Mrs. Bushkin

5. Festivus, a holiday "for the rest of us," may have been popularized on *Seinfeld* in the nineties, but WHO is said to have actually dreamed it up years earlier?
- a. *New Yorker* editor William Shawn
- b. Author Stephen King
- c. *Seinfeld* co-creator Larry David
- d. A *Reader's Digest* editor, Dan O'Keefe

SCORE FOR THIS TEST: _____ TOTAL SO FAR: _____

ANSWERS: 1. d (in *Gone with the Wind*), **2.** b, **3.** a, **4.** c, **5.** d

Do You Know **QUOTES**?

Take 10 points for each correct answer. Maximum this page: 50 points!

Match the quotes with the quote givers:

1. "When I'm good, I'm very good. But when I'm bad, I'm better."

a. Victor Borge

2. "Who put pineapple juice in my pineapple juice?"

b. Lloyd Bentsen

3. "I saw the angel in the marble and carved until I set him free."

c. W.C. Fields

4. "The Steinway people have asked me to announce that this is a Baldwin piano."

d. Mae West

5. "Senator, you're no Jack Kennedy."

e. Michelangelo

SCORE FOR THIS TEST: _____ TOTAL SO FAR: _____

Do You Know **QUOTES**?

Take 10 points for each correct answer. Maximum this page: 50 points!

More quotes to match:

1. "If you want to sacrifice the admiration
of many men for the criticism of one, go
ahead, get married."

a. Al Michaels

2. "The two most beautiful words in the
English language are 'Check enclosed.'"

b. Dorothy Parker

3. "I am prepared to wait for my answer
until Hell freezes over."

c. George H.W. Bush

4. "Do you believe in miracles?"

d. Katharine Hepburn

5. "We're going to strengthen the
American family to make them more like
the Waltons and less like the Simpsons."

e. Adlai Stevenson

SCORE FOR THIS TEST: _____ TOTAL SO FAR: _____

Answers: 1. d, 2. b, 3. e, 4. a, 5. c

Do You Know **WHAT**?

Take 20 points for each correct answer. Maximum this page: 100 points!

1. **WHAT's the traditional gift for a thirty-fifth wedding anniversary?**
   a. Pearls
   b. Coral
   c. Rubies
   d. Silk

2. **The Vietnam War anthem "Ballad of the Green Berets" was co-written and sung by Barry Sadler, a military man. WHAT was his rank?**
   a. PFC
   b. SSgt
   c. Lt
   d. Lt Col

3. **WHAT are Pippin, Gravenstein, and Northern Spy?**
   a. Varieties of tomato
   b. Varieties of apple
   c. Racetracks
   d. Record labels

4. **Count Rumford, a late-eighteenth-century physicist and heat expert, is still revered today by those who make WHAT?**
   a. Fireplaces
   b. Oral thermometers
   c. Cookstoves
   d. Gasoline engines

5. **WHAT is a Shahtoosh?**
   a. An almond pastry made in several Middle Eastern countries
   b. A Pakistani auto maker
   c. An Iranian overstuffed cushion made for a throne or large chair
   d. A shawl woven from the fine down of the endangered Tibetan antelope

SCORE FOR THIS TEST: _____ TOTAL SO FAR: _____

ANSWERS: 1. b, 2. b, 3. b, 4. a, 5. d

Do You Know **WHERE**?

Take 20 points for each correct answer. Maximum this page: 100 points!

1. Robert Stroud, the convicted murderer known as "The Birdman of Alcatraz," was so called because he cared for canaries—not at Alcatraz but at another prison he inhabited earlier. WHERE?
   a. San Quentin
   b. Leavenworth
   c. Danbury
   d. Allenwood

2. WHERE is the octagonal Castel del Monte?
   a. Sardinia
   b. Nova Scotia, Canada
   c. Puglia, Italy
   d. A Disney movie

3. WHERE might you apply Restylane?
   a. To your face, for wrinkles
   b. To your body, for fat
   c. To your wood furniture, for a high shine
   d. To your aquarium, for healthy fish

4. In a single building, both the laser and FM radio were invented and the uranium atom was split for the first time. WHERE?
   a. CIA Headquarters in Langley, Virginia
   b. A defunct private scientific research center in Colorado
   c. The Hochtechnische Schule in Bern, Switzerland
   d. Pupin Hall at Columbia University

5. Other than New York City, WHERE can you find a Guggenheim museum?
   a. Bilbao, Spain
   b. Venice, Italy
   c. Berlin, Germany
   d. Las Vegas, Nevada
   e. in all four cities

SCORE FOR THIS TEST: _____ TOTAL SO FAR: _____

Do You Know **ADVERTISING LINES**?

Take 10 points for each correct answer. Maximum this page: 50 points!

Fill in, please:

1. American Express cards: "Do you _____ _____?"

2. Clairol: "Only her hairdresser knows _____ _____."

3. Scope: "Even your best friends _____ _____ _____."

4. "Bosco gives you iron and _____ _____ _____."

5. "Mr. Clean will clean your whole house and _____ _____ _____ _____."

SCORE FOR THIS TEST: _____ TOTAL SO FAR: _____

Do You Know **WHICH—ODD ONE OUT**?

Take 10 points for each correct answer. Maximum this page: 50 points!

1. WHICH color *isn't* in the Burberry check?

- a. Tan
- b. Black
- c. Red
- d. Blue
- e. White

2. WHICH brand *won't* you find in a bicycle shop?

- a. Campagnolo
- b. Zéfal
- c. Ketel One
- d. Shimano

3. WHICH *wasn't* the name of one of Johnny Carson's wives?

- a. Joan
- b. Joanne
- c. Joanna
- d. Ann Carol
- e. Alexis

4. Three of these fit veteran actor Ricardo Montalban. WHICH one *doesn't*?

- a. Pitchman for the Chrysler Cordoba's "soft Corinthian leather"
- b. Assistant bandleader at Ricky Ricardo's Club Babalu
- c. Khan in *Star Trek: The Wrath of Khan*
- d. Mr. Roarke, host of *Fantasy Island*

5. WHICH *wasn't* the name of a big-money TV show?

- a. "The Big Surprise"
- b. "Dotto"
- c. "Dollars Galore"
- d. "Twenty-One"
- e. "The $64,000 Challenge"

SCORE FOR THIS TEST: _____ TOTAL SO FAR: _____

Do You Know **TRUE OR FALSE**?

Take 4 points for each correct answer. Maximum this page: 20 points!

1. The Frito Bandito, one-time cartoon spokes-character for Fritos corn chips, was a peaceful, unarmed fellow who surreptitiously took people's chips.
_____ True   _____ False

2. Petula Clark, who scored a giant hit with "Downtown" in 1965, retired on the royalties from that song but licensed her name and persona to another singer who continued "Petula Clark's" career.
_____ True   _____ False

3. Donatello, the tech-savvy member of the Teenage Mutant Ninja Turtles, the one who prefers to think things out before slamming people around, wears an orange mask.
_____ True   _____ False

4. There's a street named Paul Shaffer Drive, named for the shades-wearing bandleader, in his hometown of Thunder Bay, Ontario.
_____ True   _____ False

5. *Frankenstein Meets the Wolfman,* in which Wolfie finds the monster on ice and thaws him out, brought together Boris Karloff and Lon Chaney Jr.
_____ True   _____ False

SCORE FOR THIS TEST: _____ TOTAL SO FAR: _____

Do You Know **FILL-IN QUIZ**?

Take 10 points for each correct answer. Maximum this page: 50 points!

1. Loretta Lynn grew up in _____ _____, Kentucky.

2. Captain Geoffrey T. Spaulding's occupation: _____ _____.

3. Reports are that Ted Williams and Walt Disney were both _____ after they died.

4. She's strong, she's invincible, she's woman: _____ _____.

5. Between Boston and Atlanta, the baseball Braves were in _____.

SCORE FOR THIS TEST: _____ TOTAL SO FAR: _____

ANSWERS: 1. Butcher Holler, **2.** African explorer (Groucho) in *Animal Crackers*), **3.** frozen (true about Ted, false about Walt), **4.** Helen Reddy ("I Am Woman"), **5.** Milwaukee

Do You Know **WHO**?

Take 10 points for each correct answer. Maximum this page: 50 points!

1. WHO was a regular diner at the Café Boeuf?
   a. Frasier Crane
   b. Barney Hefner
   c. Garrison Keillor
   d. Sam Malone

2. WHO invented the modern classification of plants and animals?
   a. Carl Linnaeus
   b. Charles Darwin
   c. Stephen Jay Gould
   d. Scott Nearing

3. WHO founded the Avis car rental company?
   a. Warren E. Avis
   b. Harold J. Avis
   c. Margaret P. Avis
   d. No one named Avis

4. WHO was Cézanne speaking of when he called a fellow painter "only an eye, but good God, what an eye"?
   a. Cassatt
   b. Gaugin
   c. Utrillo
   d. Monet

5. WHO *wasn't* on *Peyton Place?*
   a. Ryan O'Neal
   b. Mia Farrow
   c. David Canary
   d. Tom Selleck

SCORE FOR THIS TEST: _____ TOTAL SO FAR: _____

ANSWERS: 1. c (on *A Prairie Home Companion*), **2.** a, **3.** a, **4.** d, **5.** d

Do You Know **WHAT**?

Take 10 points for each correct answer. Maximum this page: 50 points!

1. WHAT are Saturn's rings mostly composed of?
   - a. Mixed gases
   - b. Emerald dust
   - c. Ice particles
   - d. Remnants of a solar explosion

2. *The Misfits* was the first picture Marilyn Monroe and Clark Gable made together. Besides that distinction, WHAT else was special about it?
   - a. It was the last film for both of them
   - b. It was filmed entirely on Gable's estate
   - c. Except while cameras rolled, the two stars didn't speak to each other
   - d. It was filmed with no director, but a directorial committee that practiced "participatory democracy"

3. WHAT was Lucy Ricardo's maiden name?
   - a. Ball
   - b. Vance
   - c. Frawley
   - d. McGillicuddy

4. Pac-Man was originally titled WHAT?
   - a. Pizza Man
   - b. Pac v. Ghost
   - c. Paku-Paku
   - d. Puck Man

5. WHAT movie was advertised as "The Ultimate Trip"?
   - a. *Star Trek: The Motion Picture*
   - b. *Road to Morocco*
   - c. *2001: A Space Odyssey*
   - d. *The Timothy Leary Story*

SCORE FOR THIS TEST: _____ TOTAL SO FAR: _____

ANSWERS: 1. c, 2. a, 3. d, 4. d, 5. c

Do You Know **BASEBALL MINUTIAE**?

Take 10 points for each correct answer. Maximum this page: 50 points!

Match the retired baseball uniform numbers with their onetime holders:

1. Ted Williams   a. 3

2. Reggie Jackson   b. 7

3. Mickey Mantle   c. 9

4. Babe Ruth   d. 21

5. Roberto Clemente   e. 44

SCORE FOR THIS TEST: _____ TOTAL SO FAR: _____

Do You Know **WHICH—ODD ONE OUT**?

Take 10 points for each correct answer. Maximum this page: 50 points!

1. **WHICH** music hall *didn't* rock promoter Bill Graham operate?
    - b. Fillmore East
    - c. Fillmore West
    - d. Whisky a Go Go
    - e. Winterland

2. **WHICH** famed opera singer *isn't* (or *wasn't*) a soprano?
    - a. Marian Anderson
    - b. Renée Fleming
    - c. Deborah Voigt
    - d. Anna Netrebko

3. **WHICH** jazz musician *isn't* (or *wasn't*) primarily a pianist?
    - a. Art Tatum
    - b. Horace Silver
    - c. Oscar Pettiford
    - d. Ahmad Jamal

4. **WHICH** *wasn't* composed by Leonard Bernstein?
    - a. *West Side Story*
    - b. *On the Town*
    - c. *Kaddish*
    - d. *Three Places in New England*

5. **WHICH** of these notables *didn't* die in a plane crash?
    - a. John Denver
    - b. Otis Redding
    - c. Rick Nelson
    - d. John F. Kennedy, Jr.
    - e. George "Superman" Reeves
    - f. Jim Croce
    - g. Rocky Marciano
    - h. Knute Rockne
    - i. Patsy Cline
    - j. Roberto Clemente

SCORE FOR THIS TEST: _____ TOTAL SO FAR: _____

ANSWERS: 1. c, **2.** a (alto), **3.** c (bassist), **4.** d (by Charles Ives), **5.** e (shot himself to death)

Do You Know **FILL-IN QUIZ**?

Take 10 points for each correct answer. Maximum this page: 50 points!

1. Little Shirley Temple's favorite expression, delivered with a shake of the curls: "Oh, _____ _____!"

2. Movie about gold-hunting women in search of gold-bearing men, starring Marilyn Monroe, Betty Grable, and Lauren Bacall: _____ _____ _____ _____ _____.

3. "OBJECTS IN MIRROR ARE CLOSER THAN _____ _____."

4. "When better automobiles are built, _____ will build them."

5. A Massachusetts city, a Klugman character, and a Loire wine. Same word: _____.

SCORE FOR THIS TEST: _____ TOTAL SO FAR: _____

Do You Know **HORROR & SCI-FI**?

Take 20 points for each correct answer. Maximum this page: 100 points!

Match the actors to the horror or sci-fi flicks:

1. Michael Landon

    a. *The Thing from Another World*

2. James Arness

    b. *Castle of the Living Dead*

3. Donald Sutherland

    c. *House of Wax*

4. Charles Bronson

    d. *I Was a Teenage Werewolf*

5. Steve McQueen

    e. *The Blob*

SCORE FOR THIS TEST: _____ TOTAL SO FAR: _____

Do You Know **TV JOBS**?

Take 20 points for each correct answer. Maximum this page: 100 points!

Match the TV characters to their lines of work:

1. Andy Taylor   a. valet

2. Howard Cunningham   b. lumber dealer

3. John Walton   c. sheriff

4. Fred Sanford   d. junk dealer

5. Rochester   e. store owner

SCORE FOR THIS TEST: _____ **TOTAL SO FAR:** _____

Do You Know **WHERE**?

Take 10 points for each correct answer. Maximum this page: 50 points!

1. **WHERE** did the dance fad known as The Twist get its biggest push?
    a. The Cavern
    b. The Peppermint Lounge
    c. Studio 54
    d. Beverly's

3. **WHERE** did Dick Loudon (Bob Newhart) and his wife Joanna (Mary Frann) run the Stratford Inn for eight years, until, as revealed in the last episode of *Newhart,* Bob woke up from the dream?
    a. Barbados
    b. Maine
    c. Minnesota
    d. Vermont

2. **WHERE** did Lou, Mary, Murray, and, yes, Ted get the news on the air every evening?
    a. WJM
    b. WKRP
    c. WOWO
    d. KRAP

4. The man known as D.B. Cooper, the early skyjacker, became a big pop culture figure after he took a $200,000 ransom and parachuted out of a Northwest Boeing 727. **WHERE** was he eventually found?
    a. He wasn't
    b. Mexico
    c. Arizona
    d. Pennsylvania

5. **WHERE** do many characters created by Carl Banks live?
    a. Metropolis
    b. Gotham City
    c. Duckburg
    d. Fiji

SCORE FOR THIS TEST: _____ TOTAL SO FAR: _____

Do You Know **FILL-IN QUIZ**?

Take 10 points for each correct answer. Maximum this page: 50 points!

1. Best-remembered line from *When Harry Met Sally:* "_____ _____ _____ _____ _____."

2. In the days of the military draft, student deferment classification: _____.

3. Forrest Gump: "Mama always said life was like a box of _____."

4. Valspeak expression: "Grody to the _____."

5. Avril Lavigne, Joni Mitchell, Buffy Sainte-Marie, Leonard Cohen, Kate and Anna McGarrigle, k.d. lang, and Gordon Lightfoot are all _____ _____.

SCORE FOR THIS TEST: _____ TOTAL SO FAR: _____

Do You Know **QUOTES**?

Take 4 points for each correct answer. Maximum this page: 20 points!

1. "Never eat more than you can lift."

a. Ben Franklin

2. "Can it core a apple?"

b. Leona Helmsley

3. "History is more or less bunk."

c. Ed Norton

4. "Only the little people pay taxes."

d. Miss Piggy

5. "Lighthouses are more helpful
   than churches."

e. Henry Ford

SCORE FOR THIS TEST: _____ TOTAL SO FAR: _____

Do You Know **FILL-IN QUIZ**?

Take 10 points for each correct answer. Maximum this page: 50 points!

1. Clara Peller's trademark shout: "_____ _____ _____?"

2. Where to play Tetris: _____ _____.

3. Until the company was renamed Crayola, Inc., _____ & _____ made the crayons.

4. "Mr. Whipple, please don't squeeze the _____!"

5. "*Mamma mia*, that's a _____ _____!"

SCORE FOR THIS TEST: _____ TOTAL SO FAR: _____

Do You Know **FASHION AND FADS**?

Take 10 points for each correct answer. Maximum this page: 50 points!

Every entry below was big in the sixties or the seventies. For each, say which decade.

1. Mood ring: _____

2. Leisure suit: _____

3. Nehru jacket: _____

4. Toga: _____

5. Love beads: _____

6. The hustle: _____

7. Miniskirt: _____

8. Tie-dye: _____

9. Hot pants: _____

10. Pillbox hat: _____

SCORE FOR THIS TEST: _____ **TOTAL SO FAR:** _____

Do You Know **WHAT**?

Take 10 points for each correct answer. Maximum this page: 50 points!

1. WHAT was the bonus period at the end of *Password* called?
    - a. Overtime
    - b. The Lightning Round
    - c. Spin-off
    - d. The Snap

2. WHAT was the title of Clifford Irving's hoax autobiography of Howard Hughes?
    - a. *Autobiography of Howard Hughes*
    - b. *Howard—His Own Story*
    - c. *My Life, For Real*
    - d. *Up in the Air*

3. The slogan was "Dell Comics are _____ comics." WHAT kind of comics were they?
    - a. Fun
    - b. Good
    - c. Swell
    - d. Fine

4. A woman's American dress size 8 is WHAT size in Europe?
    - a. 8
    - b. 12
    - c. 42
    - d. 48

5. WHAT did James F. Blake do in Montgomery, Alabama, on December 1, 1955, that assured him a footnote in history?
    - a. Scored three holes-in-one in a single round of golf—left-handed
    - b. Told Rosa Parks to give up her bus seat to a white man
    - c. Invented the mint julep
    - d. Recorded Elvis for the first time

SCORE FOR THIS TEST: _____ TOTAL SO FAR: _____

ANSWERS: 1. b, 2. a, 3. b, 4. c, 5. b

Do You Know **TV ADDRESSES**?

Take 10 points for each correct answer. Maximum this page: 50 points!

Match the New York addresses with the TV characters who lived there:

1. Ralph and Alice

2. Lucy and Ricky

3. Felix and Oscar

4. Jerry and Cosmo

5. Archie and Edith

a. 623 East 68th Street

129 West 81st Street

c. 1049 Park Avenue

d. 704 Hauser Street

e. 328 Chauncey Street

SCORE FOR THIS TEST: _____ TOTAL SO FAR: _____

Do You Know **WHICH**?

Take 10 points for each correct answer. Maximum this page: 50 points!

1. WHICH television series had a theme song that began, "Well, I'm not the kind to kiss and tell, but I've been seen with Farrah"?
    a. *The Big Valley*
    b. *Fall Guy*
    c. *Owen Marshall: Counselor at Law*
    d. *The Six Million Dollar Man*

2. WHICH head of state shared a birthday with, and was mad about, Elvis?
    a. Jacques Chirac, president of France
    b. Golda Meir, prime minister of Israel
    c. Silvio Berlusconi, prime minister of Italy
    d. Junichiro Koizumi, prime minister of Japan

3. WHICH movie helped make The Hustle a hugely popular dance . . . for a while?
    a. *Minnesota Fats*
    b. *The Sting*
    c. *Saturday Night Fever*
    d. *Beach Blanket Bingo*

4. Milli Vanilli's cover was blown when they were lip-synching at a concert being taped for MTV and the recording got stuck and kept repeating a line. WHICH of their hit songs was the fatal tune?
    a. "Girl You Know It's True"
    b. "Girl I'm Gonna Miss You"
    c. "Blame It on the Rain"
    d. "All or Nothing"

5. Besides the New York Yankees, WHICH did Billy Martin manage?
    a. Minnesota Twins
    b. Detroit Tigers
    c. Texas Rangers
    d. Oakland Athletics
    e. all of the above

SCORE FOR THIS TEST: _____ TOTAL SO FAR: _____

ANSWERS: 1. b, 2. d, 3. c, 4. a, 5. e

Do You Know **WHAT**?

1. On *Love Boat,* Fred Grandy played the purser. Everyone called him Gopher, but the character's real name was WHAT?
   a. Adam Bricker
   b. Gordon Stubing
   c. Gary Purser
   d. Burl Smith

2. WHAT freaks out Indiana Jones?
   a. Rats
   b. Snakes
   c. Cats
   d. Enclosed spaces

3. Before he was an actor, WHAT was Mr. T?
   a. A pro football player
   b. A pro wrestler
   c. A bodyguard
   d. A grade school principal

4. In *Urban Cowboy,* WHAT does Debra Winger secretly practice?
   a. Dirty dancing
   b. Riding a mechanical bull
   c. Guitar
   d. Karaoke

5. WHAT kind of work does Marty do in the movie that bears his name?
   a. Butcher
   b. Baker
   c. Waiter
   d. Professor

SCORE FOR THIS TEST: _____ TOTAL SO FAR: _____

ANSWERS: 1. d, 2. b, 3. c, 4. b, 5. a

Do You Know **TV CATCHPHRASES**?

Take 10 points for each correct answer. Maximum this page: 50 points!

Four trademark expressions, five names. That's because two of these folks used the same catchphrase. Match, please:

1. Jack Paar   **a.** "Ibi-da"

2. Lurch   **b.** "You rang?"

3. Mork   **c.** "I kid you not"

4. Maynard G. Krebs   **d.** "Nanu-nanu"

5. Latka Gravas

SCORE FOR THIS TEST: _____ TOTAL SO FAR: _____

ANSWERS: 1. c (*The Tonight Show, The Jack Paar Show*), **2.** b (*The Addams Family*), **3.** d (*Mork & Mindy*), **4.** b (*The Many Loves of Dobie Gillis*), **5.** a (*Taxi*)

Do You Know **TV CATCHPHRASES**?

Take 4 points for each correct answer. Maximum this page: 20 points!

Five more from television:

1. "And that's the way it was."

a. Flo Castleberry

2. "That was so funny I forgot to laugh."

b. Maude Findlay

3. "Kiss my grits!"

c. Walter Cronkite

4. "And you are . . . ?"

d. Lisa Loopner

5. "God'll get you for that, Walter."

e. David Spade

SCORE FOR THIS TEST: _____ TOTAL SO FAR: _____

Do You Know **THE MARX BROTHERS**?

Take 10 points for each correct answer. Maximum this page: 50 points!

Match the Marx Brothers with their real first names:

1. Chico   a. Julius

2. Harpo   b. Herbert

3. Groucho   c. Milton

4. Gummo   d. Arthur

5. Zeppo   e. Leonard

SCORE FOR THIS TEST: _____ TOTAL SO FAR: _____

Do You Know **BANDLEADERS**?

Take 10 points for each correct answer. Maximum this page: 50 points!

Match the bandleaders to their instruments:

1. Tommy Dorsey

a. saxophone

2. Jimmy Dorsey

b. piano

3. Glenn Miller

c. clarinet

4. Fletcher Henderson

d. trombone

5. Artie Shaw

e. trombone

SCORE FOR THIS TEST: _____ TOTAL SO FAR: _____

ANSWERS: 1. d, **2.** a, **3.** e, **4.** b, **5.** c

Do You Know **FILL-IN QUIZ**?

Take 10 points for each correct answer. Maximum this page: 50 points!

1. Pedro, the head-only pal of Spanish ventriloquist Señor Wences, always growled "'S awright!" And he lived _____ _____ _____.

2. Magazine created by "The Usual Gang of Idiots": _____.

3. TV personality prominently referenced in the movie *Rainman:* Judge _____.

4. William E. Miller and Curtis LeMay both wanted to be _____ _____.

5. "Tan me hide when I'm _____, _____."

SCORE FOR THIS TEST: _____ TOTAL SO FAR: _____

ANSWERS: 1. in a box, **2.** *Mad*, **3.** Wapner (of *The People's Court*, Raymond Babbitt's very, very favorite program), **4.** vice president (Miller ran with Goldwater '64, LeMay with Wallace '68), **5.** dead, Fred (from the song "Tie Me Kangaroo Down")

Do You Know **NAMES**?

Take 10 points for each correct answer. Maximum this page: 50 points!

Celebrities on the left, their earlier names on the right. Match:

1. Jerry Lewis

a. Declan MacManus

2. Anna Nicole Smith

b. Walden Cassotto

3. Elvis Costello

c. Vickie Lynn Hogan

4. Bobby Darin

d. Lucille Fay Le Sueur

5. Joan Crawford

e. Joseph Levitch

SCORE FOR THIS TEST: _____ TOTAL SO FAR: _____

Do You Know **FILL-IN QUIZ**?

Take 10 points for each correct answer. Maximum this page: 50 points!

1. *Jaws* police chief: "You're gonna need a bigger _____."

2. *Candid Camera* began life on radio as _____ _____.

3. "A census taker once tried to test me. I ate his liver with some fava beans and _____ _____ _____."

4. Over the decades, hosted by Art Baker, Jack Smith, and Rich Little: _____ _____.

5. On April 23, 1985, the soft drink world was turned upside down with the introduction of _____ _____,

SCORE FOR THIS TEST: _____ TOTAL SO FAR: _____

Do You Know **TV CATCHPHRASES**?

Take 4 points for each correct answer. Maximum this page: 20 points!

Match these catchphrases:

1. "Dy-no-mite!"   a. Geraldine

2. "Jane, you ignorant slut!"   b. Kojak

3. "Mom always liked you best."   c. J.J.

4. "What you see is what you get."   d. Dan Aykroyd

5. "Who loves ya, baby?"   e. Tom Smothers

SCORE FOR THIS TEST: _____ TOTAL SO FAR: _____

Do You Know **WHERE**?

Take 10 points for each correct answer. Maximum this page: 50 points!

1. WHERE did Lyndon B. Johnson vacation?
- a. The Ladybird Ranch
- b. The LBJ Ranch
- c. Birdland
- d. The Bar B Ranch

2. WHERE was Adolf Eichmann, the high-level Nazi manager, captured?
- a. Argentina
- b. Brazil
- c. Israel
- d. Poland

3. The lead characters in *Starsky and Hutch* were detectives operating WHERE?
- a. Southern California
- b. San Francisco
- c. Chicago
- d. Miami

4. On *Mork and Mindy,* WHERE was Mork from?
- a. The planet Bork
- b. The planet Ork
- c. The planet Nanu
- d. The universe Dawber

5. WHERE did Elvis serve most of his stint in the Army?
- a. Pearl Harbor, Hawaii
- b. Kuwait
- c. Stuttgart, Germany
- d. Friedberg, Germany

SCORE FOR THIS TEST: _____ TOTAL SO FAR: _____

Do You Know **FILL-IN QUIZ**?

Take 10 points for each correct answer. Maximum this page: 50 points!

1. In 1981, the U.S. Department of Agriculture declared that, as far as school lunches go, ketchup is a _____.

2. As teenagers, they started imitating musical instruments as they sang: trumpet, trombone, ukulele. The sound was different. It worked, and they had a career for decades. They were The _____ Brothers.

3. Kent with the _____ filter.

4. Pitchwoman for Comet cleanser: _____ the Plumber.

5. GL-70 and Floristan were ingredients in two brands of _____.

SCORE FOR THIS TEST: _____ TOTAL SO FAR: _____

Do You Know **FILL-IN QUIZ**?

Take 20 points for each correct answer. Maximum this page: 100 points!

1. In the movie *Sixteen Candles,* Sam (Molly Ringwald) gives geeky Ted (Anthony Michael Hall) a pair of her _____.

2. Actor father of actors Jeff and Beau: _____.

3. Focus of the movie *Titanic:* "The _____ of the _____."

4. Leah Berliawsky was better known as the abstract expressionist sculptor

_____ _____.

5. Olympian decathlon gold medalist and Wheaties box star Bruce Jenner was briefly married to Elvis's one-time Graceland roommate, _____ _____.

SCORE FOR THIS TEST: _____ TOTAL SO FAR: _____

ANSWERS: 1. underpants, **2.** Lloyd (Bridges), **3.** "The Heart of the Ocean" (a blue diamond necklace), **4.** Louise Nevelson, **5.** Linda Thompson

Do You Know **GRAB BAG**?

Take 20 points for each correct answer. Maximum this page: 100 points!

1. Who's older, Uncle Ben or Aunt Jemima?

2. At the start of the song "One For My Baby and One More For the Road," what time is it?

3. Who is Dorothy Gale?

4. Who called what year an *"annus horribilis"*—and why?

5. Major league baseball has had a star pitcher nicknamed Dazzy and two called Dizzy. Name them all.

SCORE FOR THIS TEST: _____ TOTAL SO FAR: _____

ANSWERS: 1. Jemima (she goes back to before 1900. Ben was a World War II baby), **2.** "It's quarter to three" ("there's no one in the place except you and me . . ."), **3.** Dorothy of Kansas and Oz, of course, **4.** Queen Elizabeth II said it of 1992, because, for starters, Prince Andrew and Sarah Ferguson separated, a tabloid published a photo of Sarah topless, Princess Anne divorced, Windsor Castle suffered a fire, **5.** Dazzy Vance, Dizzy Dean, Dizzy Trout

Do You Know **GRAB BAG**?

Take 100 points for each correct answer. Maximum this page: 500 points!

Here's one final opportunity to bump up your score with some big-point answers:

1. Where did Butch Cavendish and his gang operate?

2. Who recorded *Top 40 of the Lord?*

3. "The body's not cold yet." "I'll fix that—I'll phone for service . . . [on phone] Send up enough ice to cool a warm body." Who said it?

4. Mr. Kenneth, the hairdresser who gave Jackie Kennedy her bouffant—his last name, please?

5. Name all seven Disney dwarfs.

SCORE FOR THIS TEST: _____ TOTAL SO FAR: _____

ANSWERS: 1. Texas (they were the bad guys who ambushed the Texas Rangers unit including the one who became The Lone Ranger), **2.** Sha Na Na ("Are you on the top 40 of your lordy-lordy-lordy?"), **3.** Chico Marx (in *Room Service*), **4.** Bartelle, **5.** (in alphabetical order) Bashful, Doc, Dopey, Grumpy, Happy, Sleepy, Sneezy

What Your Score Means

Maximum possible score is 8,380 points. A perfect grade is very, very unlikely, but for everybody else, here's how to rate your performance:

Above 8,000:   Spectacular! Truly spectacular!
6,500–8,000:   A real good showing—better than most.
4,000–6,499:   Respectable, if nothing to boast about.
Below 4,000:   At least you've probably learned a bit along the way.

Did a question in this book remind you of some bit of information that would make a great trivia question? Use this page to jot down your own favorites.